SUNDAY SUPPERS

Southern Living

SUNDAY SUPPERS

Simple, Delicious Menus for Family Gatherings

CYNTHIA GRAUBART

Oxmoor
House

Published by Oxmoor House, an imprint of Time Inc. Books
225 Liberty Street, New York, NY 10281

Senior Editor: Katherine Cobbs
Editor: Meredith L. Butcher
Project Editor: Lacie Pinyan
Photo Director: Paden Reich
Designers: Claire Cormany, Maribeth Jones
Photographers: Time Inc. Food Studios
Prop Stylists: Time Inc. Food Studios
Food Stylists: Time Inc. Food Studios
Assistant Production Director: Sue Chodakiewicz
Senior Production Manager: Greg A. Amason
Copy Editor: Cathy Fowler
Proofreaders: Norma Butterworth-McKittrick, Julie Gillis
Indexer: Carol Roberts

ISBN-13: 978-0-8487-5513-3

Library of Congress Control Number: 2017942367

First Edition 2017

Printed in China

10 9 8 7 6 5 4 3 2 1

We welcome your comments and suggestions about Time Inc. Books.
Please write to us at:
Time Inc. Books
Attention: Book Editors
P.O. Box 62310
Tampa, Florida 33662-2310

Time Inc. Books products may be purchased for business or promotional use. For information on bulk purchases, please contact Christi Crowley in the Special Sales Department at (845) 895-9858.

Contributing Photographers: Iain Bagwell, page 239; Sharon Brody, 261; Justin Fox Burks, page 215; Timothy L. Hall, page 129; Andrew Thomas Lee, page 45; Tracey Lee, page 153; Dustin Lewis, page 189; Adrian Miller, page 83

CONTENTS

Introduction

SUNDAY SUPPERS have always been special in my family, even if they were not laborious gastronomic feasts. We mark the end of the weekend with this casual meal, often eating a little earlier (it's a school night after all) and many times including another family at our table. The atmosphere is always relaxed, and no one wants the day—or the weekend—to end. And the food is always good. How could it not be with our vast array of agricultural riches? Just-picked flavorful produce, fresh seafood, and meats and poultry of every kind remind us just how good it is to be a Southerner.

Historically, Sunday "supper" in the South was a light meal at the end of the day. Sunday "dinner" was the big meal of the day, shared with nearby family and friends and served around noon or after church. My grandmother's sideboard always held an impressive array of vegetables—greens beans, corn, sliced tomatoes, potato salad, and more. A ham, beef roast, or chicken took center stage, and to top it all off, a dessert display promised a sugar high followed by a glorious crash into an afternoon nap.

Today my Sunday "dinners" are enjoyed on special occasions and might be a late brunch, sometimes in a restaurant or eaten at home in the traditional style served at midday. But it's a rare occurrence. Most of the time, it's just a quick sandwich or other light bite before we head out for an afternoon of activities or chores.

It's our Sunday "suppers," served in the evening, that are sometimes a full meal, sometimes a soup and sandwich, but always all about family. If your family is struggling to find time to eat together regularly, Sunday supper is a great place to start. We have more time to spend cooking on Sundays, and it doesn't have to be fancy. Family mealtime is heralded by educators, clergy, and grandmothers as an important part of a child's growth and development. Some studies even suggest that gathering regularly at the table is an influential behavior that contributes to higher grades in school, increased vocabulary, and more.

My Sunday suppers of the winter season are celebrated with one-pot meals of soup or stew, big roasts, and hearty vegetables. In summer, the menu changes to lighter, easier, and more casual food. The meal has a different rhythm, and we often eat outdoors for a picnic or barbecue. Fresh, light salads are brimming with savory garden vegetables, and summer fruits star as dessert. And no matter the season, I'm always looking for leftovers that will provide for a quick-cook meal for Monday night. You'll find a variety of seasonal meals and cooking methods—there's something here for everyone.

We all know Monday morning arrives soon enough, so we savor this time around the table before the new week begins and the treadmill of life gains daily momentum. Even when the meal has finished, we might linger at the table in conversation, still picking at the crunchy seasoned bits of the end of a roast, or enjoying another small spoonful of corn soufflé. My mother would often grab the honey jar and bring it to the table at the end of the meal, and we would sit and eat the leftover biscuits with rivers of dripping honey. It's one of my fondest memories from childhood. I hope this book will help you make special mealtime memories, too.

HOW TO USE THIS BOOK

Although this book is written in menus, the recipes are easily exchanged between menus. Each menu presents three recipes as a jumping-off point. Add other recipes as needed to complete the menu as you see fit. Sometimes all that's needed is a salad. The note at the beginning of the menu gives a clue as to the tastes and textures you'll find in the recipes, plus a bit of preparation strategy. I hope you'll write in this book, recording the new menus you create and the changes you make in a recipe. It's a sign of a well-loved cookbook when the cook records successes, failures, tips, and notes on the recipes they've used. Cookbooks begin as teaching tools but become diaries of family meals and fond memories.

HOW TO READ A RECIPE

Success in the kitchen depends on many factors, and it begins with how you read the recipe. A well-written recipe is a roadmap, complete with clear directions and important commentary along the route. After all, the writer is rooting for your success! Start by reading through the recipe twice (all the words!). Check the ingredients—do you have everything on hand? Check the equipment— do you have the right sized pans? An electric hand mixer? Sometimes underlining the verbs helps make sure you have all the tools you need. What about the timing? Are there overnight marinating times, long rises, or resting times? Room-temperature ingredients? Lots of hands-on time? Do you have enough time to make this recipe?

CREATING A MENU

This book is written in a menu format to aid the cook in putting dishes together, but it's not the only way to approach the book. Pulling recipes from multiple menus to create your own is easy to do. Often I look at the main course first: Am I serving a large meat-loving crowd, or do I need something lighter for a small family meal? Let's say I've selected *Rosemary-Garlic Chicken Quarters (page 148)* as my main course. Next I choose my side dishes, looking at taste, texture, color, season, and even weather. Since I usually serve a beet salad as a side with this recipe in the winter, I think I'll serve *Okra and Tomatoes (page 74)* for something a little different in summer weather. When I read the directions for the chicken, I was reminded that it's made in a slow cooker, so it won't be fighting for any stovetop time from the okra. And as I checked that the recipes serve the appropriate number, I saw that I'll need to double the okra recipe to even them up. For dessert, I'll make *Easy Berry Cobbler (page 107)*. It's easily assembled and bakes in the oven. Even without mixing and matching like this, you have 52 menus in this book!

SUBSTITUTIONS AND CREATIVITY

New cooks are often nervous when wanting to make a substitution in a recipe. But the recipes here are very forgiving—there's quite a bit of wiggle room for making changes. For instance, look at the *Hot Bacon Potato Salad with Green Beans* recipe *(page 16)*. I don't have green beans on hand, but I do have some Brussels sprouts. Consider the following when making a substitution: What is the ingredient adding to the recipe? Does it contribute to the texture? To the color? Is the ingredient dense? Thin or thick? Solid or liquid? Is it sweet, salty, savory, or spicy? Often these answers will lead you to a good substitution. Since the green beans are prepared separately from the potatoes, I think chopping the Brussels sprouts into quarters and steaming them a few minutes will create a compatible substitution for the beans. And the sprouts love to be paired with bacon.

What if you see two recipes for a dish and you want to take some of the ingredients from one and combine them with ingredients from the other? Bravo! You are on your way to really making a recipe your own. But how do you do it? Let's say you like both the *Cucumber and Sugar Snap Salad (page 230)* and the *Sugar Snap Pea Salad (page 196)*, but you prefer the oil and vinegar in the second salad and adore the cucumber, radishes, and feta cheese in the first salad. No problem. The cucumber would easily substitute for the cauliflower, and we know from other recipes we've read and tasted that cucumbers, radishes, and feta are all at home with the other ingredients, even the oil and vinegar.

MAKING AHEAD

No organizational strategy beats "making ahead." It's every successful cook's secret weapon, and it's the only thing that can save a cook's sanity when timing is important. So many different types of dishes can be made ahead. Even "making ahead" has different applications. Some dishes, such as many vegetable dishes, can be made a little early and left at room temperature, then quickly reheated before serving. Some recipes are made in stages and can be finished off at the last minute or can be prepared to a certain point a day or two ahead before finishing. Other recipes are completely make-ahead and are cooled and frozen until needed. A good recipe will mention if all or part of the recipe can be made ahead.

REHEATING

Having a well-stocked freezer is a boon to every cook, but reheating can be a little tricky. Typically I defrost most cooked dishes at half power in the microwave oven at 1-minute intervals. If the food is dense, I'll start with 3 or 4 minutes and continue incrementally, stirring each time to note the progress. For soups and stews, I'll transfer the partially defrosted dish from the microwave to a pot on the stove and heat thoroughly until the food is a uniform 165 degrees. For casseroles, I often defrost for a day in the refrigerator, then transfer to the oven to bake. For reheating refrigerated leftovers, a sprinkling of cold water on the food before reheating in the microwave can improve the texture of the dish, particularly for pasta dishes or when reheating vegetables in a hot skillet. Whether your dish was prepared for the freezer, or you are reheating refrigerated leftovers, always bring the food up to a uniform 165 degrees before serving to conform with food safety guidelines. And if you are unsure about the safety of any food, remember "when in doubt, throw it out."

LOOKING FOR LEFTOVERS

Double-duty is a great strategy for meal planning, so always keep an eye out for what will be left over from a meal. But even without a recipe, bits of "extras" can be reinvented for another meal. When stirred into rice for a casserole or into mashed potatoes for potato cakes, leftover meats, vegetables, and grains can come together in new ways for a stir-fry, sandwich, or omelet. My children would eat anything I put in a tortilla!

PANTRY

Pantry staples become highly personal over time but should always include broths and stocks, beans and grains, condiments—both savory and sweet—and herbs and spices. I have a number of "pantry meals" I can make at a moment's notice with what I have on hand. My freezer holds homemade stocks, frozen fruits and vegetables, and several fully-cooked dinners that I rotate into my weekly meal planning. Attach a permanent marker to the inside of a kitchen cabinet or the side of the fridge to write a name and a date on everything going into the freezer. No more soup bones masquerading as a meal.

FAVORITE KITCHEN TOOLS

My microplane grater has to be my favorite kitchen tool. From zesting citrus fruits to grating hard cheeses, I reach for this tool nearly every day. To reduce the chances of a slip, hold the grater horizontally across the rim of a bowl and move the ingredient being grated, but not the grater.

Slow cookers have a dedicated place in my kitchen, and I own several. We all have times when having dinner waiting on us when we get home is the best part of our day. A 6-quart slow cooker is best for a family. Now as an empty nester, I often use a 3½-quart model.

Oven thermometers are often overlooked, but can truly make a dramatic difference in the outcome of a dish. I had convinced myself I was a terrible baker because nothing ever turned out the way that the recipe said it should. My confidence was restored after I discovered that my oven ran nearly 40 degrees too cool! It's a small investment to increase your success. Instant-read thermometers are affordable and always reassuring when checking for doneness of beef and chicken.

MENU

Preparing a menu where all the dishes are ready to serve at the same time is a bit of an art. The good news is that the outcome always improves with practice. There are some basic strategies that will make this task easier. In the recipe-reading phase of menu planning, look for any clues the author has provided for you—can this recipe be made ahead? How far? Frozen ahead? This lets you know how much in advance that dish can be prepared. Gather the recipes and make a time chart. I always work backward from the particular time I want to serve the meal. Using the menu on page 174, here's my time chart:

7:00 pm
SUPPER IS SERVED, CARVE ROAST AT THE TABLE

6:30 pm
REMOVE ROAST FROM OVEN

6:15 pm
PREPARE VEGETABLE HASH

5:30 pm
PUT ROAST IN TO BAKE

5:00 pm
PREHEAT OVEN AND MAKE HERB RUB

4:30 pm
LET ROAST STAND AT ROOM TEMP ONE HOUR; SET TABLE

Morning of Gathering
BAKE CAKE AND REFRIGERATE UNTIL SERVING

Chapter 1

JUST US

For many of our Sundays throughout the year, it's "just us." And often that's just right. Setting aside some family time for Sunday supper can be simple, or it can be livened up with extra hands in the kitchen. It can also be a good opportunity to set a more formal table to give the kids a little practice learning table manners, especially the kind Grandma wants to see at the holiday table.

I've gathered a variety of dishes for supper. Some are quick-fix, such as our *Tomato and Feta Shrimp,* or nearly hands-off, as with our *Slow-Cooker Pork.* And our desserts are extra special: Try the *Mud Pie Meringue Sundaes, Sumptuous Swoon Pies,* or *Homemade Marshmallows.*

In our family, we would strive to have homework nearly finished before Sunday supper (especially the hands-on projects that took up considerable space on the dining table) so that we could create a relaxed atmosphere. During the meal, we woud talk of what we were looking forward to in the coming week, or muse over the outcome of sports games. Discussing social ills and solving world problems were all fair game. Those mealtimes are some of my favorite memories.

MENU ONE

SERVES 6

**BRAISED
SHORT RIBS** (PAGE 15)

**HOT BACON POTATO
SALAD WITH GREEN
BEANS** (PAGE 16)

**MISSISSIPPI MUD
CUPCAKES** (PAGE 17)

Bone-in meats are more tender and flavorful than boneless, and these beef short ribs are no exception. The marinade further ensures tenderness, and the browning of the flour-dredged ribs produces a rich, deep-flavored sauce. Classic potato salad ingredients, with the addition of bacon and green beans, go hand in hand with the lusty short ribs. Sinfully delicious chocolate cupcakes round out this hearty meat-and-potatoes menu.

Plan ahead to allow time to marinate the ribs and for the three hours of braising in the oven. Cook the potatoes any time during the day. You can blanch the greens beans in advance, as well. Refrigerate them separately. When ready to serve, reheat them separately too. Follow the recipe directions to prepare the dressing, and then combine the ingredients. (Adding the vinegar too far ahead of time will turn the green beans an unappealing shade of gray-green.) The cupcakes can be made and refrigerated up to two days in advance.

Braised
SHORT RIBS

Serves 6   Hands-on 35 minutes   Total 7 hours, 35 minutes

2 ¼ cups dry red wine
2 ¼ cups beef broth
2 garlic cloves, chopped
1 teaspoon ground allspice
½ teaspoon ground ginger
4 pounds beef short ribs, trimmed and cut in half
1 teaspoon salt
1 teaspoon freshly ground black pepper
½ cup all-purpose flour
3 tablespoons olive oil
1 carrot, chopped
½ onion, chopped
1 celery rib, chopped
2 tablespoons tomato paste

1. Combine ¼ cup wine, ¼ cup broth, garlic, allspice, and ginger in a shallow dish; add ribs, turning to coat. Cover and chill ribs for 4 to 6 hours, turning occasionally.

2. Remove ribs from marinade, reserving marinade. Sprinkle ribs with salt and pepper; dredge in flour.

3. Cook ribs, in batches, in hot oil in a Dutch oven over medium-high heat 15 minutes or until browned. Remove ribs, and set aside.

4. Reduce heat to medium; add carrot, onion, and celery, and sauté 7 minutes or until browned. Add tomato paste; cook, stirring constantly, 3 minutes.

5. Preheat oven to 300°F. Return ribs to Dutch oven. Stir in reserved marinade and remaining 2 cups wine and 2 cups broth; bring mixture to a boil, and tightly cover.

6. Bake at 300°F for 3 hours. Remove ribs.

7. Skim fat from sauce and discard; simmer sauce for 12 to 15 minutes or until reduced by half.

Hot Bacon
POTATO SALAD
with Green Beans

Serves 8   *Hands-on 30 minutes*   *Total 30 minutes*

3 pounds fingerling potatoes, cut in half
1 (8-ounce) package haricots verts (French green beans)
½ cup white wine vinegar
1 shallot, minced
3 tablespoons honey
1 tablespoon Dijon mustard
1½ teaspoons salt
1 teaspoon freshly ground black pepper
½ cup olive oil
2 tablespoons chopped fresh dill
¼ cup coarsely chopped fresh parsley
4 fully cooked bacon slices, chopped

1. Bring potatoes and water to cover to a boil in a large Dutch oven over medium-high heat, and cook 20 minutes or until tender. Drain.

2. Meanwhile, cook green beans in boiling water to cover in a medium saucepan 3 to 4 minutes or until crisp-tender. Plunge in ice water to stop the cooking process; drain.

3. Whisk together vinegar and next 5 ingredients in a medium bowl. Add oil in a slow, steady stream, whisking constantly, until smooth.

4. Pour vinegar mixture over potatoes. Just before serving, add green beans, dill, and parsley, and toss gently until blended. Sprinkle with bacon. Serve immediately.

APPLE CRISP

Serves 8   Hands-on 15 minutes   Total 1 hour, 25 minutes

3 ounces all-purpose flour (about ⅔ cup)
¾ cup packed brown sugar
½ cup old-fashioned rolled oats
2 teaspoons ground cinnamon
¼ teaspoon salt
Dash of freshly ground nutmeg (optional)
6 tablespoons chilled butter, cut into pieces
7 cups sliced peeled Fuji apple
1 teaspoon grated lemon rind
1 tablespoon fresh lemon juice
¼ cup granulated sugar
Cooking spray

1. Preheat oven to 400°F. Weigh or lightly spoon flour into dry measuring cups; level with a knife. Combine flour, brown sugar, oats, 1 teaspoon cinnamon, salt, and, if desired, nutmeg, in a bowl. Add butter; beat at low speed with an electric mixer 3 minutes or until moist and crumbly.

2. Place apple in a large bowl; sprinkle with lemon rind and lemon juice, and toss well. Sprinkle with granulated sugar and remaining 1 teaspoon cinnamon; toss well. Spoon apple mixture into an 8-inch square glass or ceramic baking dish coated with cooking spray. Sprinkle brown sugar mixture over apple mixture. Bake, uncovered, at 400°F for 15 minutes. Reduce oven temperature to 350°F.

3. Bake an additional 40 to 50 minutes or until apples are tender and topping is crisp and brown. Let stand 15 minutes before serving.

MENU THREE

SERVES 6

SUNDAY
POT ROAST (PAGE 23)

CREAMY MUSHROOM
GRITS (PAGE 24)

PEACH-HONEY
ICEBOX PIE (PAGE 25)

This rich and flavorful Sunday pot roast is browned in bacon drippings and left to slow cook with garlic, leeks, carrots, and parsnips. A platter full of Creamy Mushroom Grits is the perfect bed upon which to serve the pot roast. Begin the preparation of this menu early in the day as the pot roast cooks for 8 to 10 hours, plus time for browning. Follow with the Peach-Honey Icebox Pie—the peaches cool for an hour and the pie freezes for 6 hours before serving. It will be worth the wait. And don't be afraid to use frozen peaches if it's not peach season. They are a fine taste of summer any time of the year. The grits can be made ahead and reheated or made about an hour before serving and kept warm.

Sunday
POT ROAST

Serves 8   *Hands-on 30 minutes*   *Total 10 hours, 30 minutes*

6 medium leeks
4 thick bacon slices
1 (4- to 4 ½-pound) boneless chuck roast, trimmed
2 teaspoons freshly ground black pepper
1 ½ teaspoons kosher salt
2 tablespoons olive oil
3 garlic cloves, minced
⅓ cup firmly packed light brown sugar
1 cup dry red wine
⅓ cup balsamic vinegar
1 pound carrots, cut into 4-inch sticks
1 pound parsnips, cut into 4-inch sticks
1 cup chicken broth
1 tablespoon cornstarch

1. Remove and discard root ends and dark green tops of leeks. Cut a slit lengthwise, and rinse thoroughly under cold running water to remove grit and sand. Place leeks in a lightly greased 5- to 6-quart slow cooker.

2. Cook bacon in a large skillet over medium heat 6 to 8 minutes or until crisp. Remove bacon, and drain on paper towels, reserving 3 tablespoons hot drippings in skillet. Crumble bacon.

3. Sprinkle roast with pepper and salt. Add olive oil to hot drippings in skillet. Place roast in skillet, and cook over medium-high heat 2 to 3 minutes on each side or until browned. Transfer roast to slow cooker, reserving 1 tablespoon drippings in skillet.

4. Add garlic to hot drippings, and sauté 30 seconds. Add brown sugar, stirring until sugar melts. Add wine and balsamic vinegar, and cook 2 minutes, stirring to loosen particles from bottom of skillet. Pour mixture over roast, and top with carrots and parsnips.

5. Cover and cook on LOW 8 to 10 hours or until meat shreds easily with a fork.

6. Transfer roast to a cutting board; cut into large chunks, removing any large pieces of fat. Transfer roast and vegetables to a platter, and keep warm.

7. Skim fat from juices in slow cooker, and transfer juices to a 2-quart saucepan. Add broth, and bring to a boil over medium-high heat. Stir together cornstarch and 2 tablespoons water in a small bowl until smooth; add to pan, stirring until blended. Boil 1 minute. Add salt and pepper to taste. Serve gravy with roast and vegetables over Creamy Mushroom Grits. Top with crumbled bacon.

Creamy Mushroom
GRITS

Serves 6   Hands-on 10 minutes   Total 20 minutes

¼ cup butter
2 (3.5-ounce) packages shiitake mushrooms, stemmed and sliced
1 cup quick-cooking yellow grits
½ cup freshly grated Parmesan cheese
1 teaspoon kosher salt
½ teaspoon freshly ground black pepper
¼ cup chopped fresh flat-leaf parsley

Melt butter in a medium skillet over medium-high heat; add mushrooms. Sauté 3 to 4 minutes or until mushrooms begin to brown. Prepare grits according to package directions. Stir in Parmesan cheese, kosher salt, and pepper. Stir in mushrooms and parsley.

Peach–Honey
ICEBOX PIE

Serves 8   *Hands-on 17 minutes*   *Total 7 hours, 32 minutes*

¼ cup butter
2½ cups chopped fresh or frozen peaches, thawed
¼ cup plus 3 tablespoons good-quality local honey
1 tablespoon fresh lemon juice
2 cups vanilla ice cream, softened
1 (9-inch) ready-made graham cracker piecrust
1 cup whipping cream

1. Melt butter in a large skillet over medium heat. Add peaches and ¼ cup honey; cook, stirring often, 6 minutes or until peaches have softened and liquid has thickened to a syrup that coats peaches. Spoon peach mixture into a medium bowl; place over a bowl of ice, and stir occasionally until cool (about 1 hour). Stir in lemon juice.

2. Add vanilla ice cream to peach mixture; stir well. Spoon ice-cream mixture into crust, spreading evenly. Cover and freeze 6 hours or until firm.

3. Let pie stand at room temperature 15 minutes before serving. Meanwhile, beat whipping cream at high speed with an electric mixer until stiff peaks form. Spoon whipped cream over pie, and drizzle with remaining 3 tablespoons honey.

Variation

VANILLA WAFER CRUST:
Preheat oven to 350°F. Stir together 2½ cups crushed vanilla wafers, ¼ cup powdered sugar, and ½ cup melted butter; firmly press on bottom, up sides, and onto lip of a lightly greased 9-inch pie plate. Bake at 350°F for 10 to 12 minutes or until golden brown. Remove from oven, and cool completely (about 1 hour). Make filling as above.

MENU FOUR

SERVES 6

Serve this homey chicken casserole when a dose of comfort is in order. The Fresh Herb Spoon Rolls take just 20 minutes of hands-on time. Bursting with cherries and covered in a buttery almond topping, the Tart Cherry Crisp, served hot or at room temperature, is a great way to enjoy the first cherries of the season. Both the crisp and the casserole can be made ahead and reheated before serving. Be sure to let the casserole rest after baking. Prepare the rolls last, as they are best served piping hot with lots of butter.

FALL CHICKEN
CASEROLE (page 29)

FRESH HERB
SPOON ROLLS (page 30)

TART CHERRY CRISP (page 32)

SET THE
SCENE

The most important piece of furniture in my home is the family table. I like to think of all of the life events it has witnessed.

From sharing supper with a date to planning a vacation, my table has supported my adventures. From listening to a sales pitch for the new roof to doing taxes, my table has held steady even when I was not. It has held up many science experiments and school projects. From nightly homework to planning for college, it has been a strong supporter of education. It has supported the elbows of young children and retired grandparents, and my teenagers' squirmy dates have sat nervously in its chairs. I look forward to the day when I have a grandchild who will smear peas on it.

Family mealtime at the table is as important as all of those other uses for the table. It's the first place children learn table manners and conversation. It's so easy to fall into a trap of discussing bad behavior, grades, and other scoldings. Make your table a safe place to discuss important topics and also a joyful place to celebrate all the good. Caring about others, taking turns in conversation, consoling over losses, and celebrating successes are all worthy endeavors for children to take part in at the table.

This menu will warm up any fall Sunday supper, and I hope it inspires you to linger a little longer at the table.

Fall Chicken
CASSEROLE

Serves 6   Hands-on 1 hour   Total 1 hour, 40 minutes

½ cup butter
6 skinned and boned chicken breasts
3 shallots, chopped
2 garlic cloves, minced
1 pound assorted fresh mushrooms, coarsely chopped
¼ cup sherry
3 tablespoons all-purpose flour
2 (14-ounce) cans chicken broth
1 (6-ounce) package long-grain and wild rice mix
½ cup grated Parmesan cheese
2 tablespoons chopped fresh flat-leaf parsley
1 tablespoon chopped fresh sage
½ teaspoon salt
½ teaspoon freshly ground black pepper
½ cup sliced toasted almonds

1. Preheat oven to 375°F. Melt 1 tablespoon butter in a large skillet over medium-high heat; add half of chicken, and cook 3 minutes or until browned; turn and cook 1 minute. Transfer to a plate. (Chicken will not be cooked completely.) Repeat procedure with 1 tablespoon butter and remaining chicken. Wipe skillet clean.

2. Melt 2 tablespoons butter in skillet over medium-high heat. Add shallots, and sauté 3 minutes or until translucent. Add garlic, and sauté 30 seconds. Add mushrooms; cook, stirring often, 4 to 5 minutes or until tender. Stir in sherry, and cook, stirring often, 1 minute.

3. Melt remaining ¼ cup butter in a 3-quart saucepan over medium-high heat. Whisk in flour; cook, whisking constantly, 1 minute. Gradually whisk in broth. Bring to a boil, whisking constantly, and cook, whisking constantly, 1 to 2 minutes or until slightly thickened. Remove from heat, and add rice (reserve flavor packet for another use), next 5 ingredients, and shallot mixture. Spoon into a lightly greased 13- x 9-inch baking dish. Top with chicken.

4. Bake at 375°F for 30 to 35 minutes or until a meat thermometer inserted in thickest portion of chicken registers 165°F. Remove from oven, and let stand 10 minutes. Sprinkle with almonds.

Fresh Herb
SPOON ROLLS

Makes 2 dozen   *Hands-on 20 minutes*   *Total 45 minutes*

1 (¼-ounce) envelope active dry yeast
2 cups warm water (110°F)
4 cups self-rising flour
¾ cup melted butter
¾ cup chopped fresh chives
½ cup chopped fresh parsley
¼ cup sugar
1 large egg, lightly beaten

1. Preheat oven to 400°F. Combine yeast and 2 cups warm water in a large bowl; let stand 5 minutes. Stir in flour and remaining ingredients. Spoon batter into 2 lightly greased 12-cup muffin pans, filling three-fourths full.

2. Bake at 400°F for 20 to 22 minutes or until golden brown.

SOUTHERN SAVVY
SILENCE IS GOLDEN

At least where cell phones are concerned. Clever hosts and parents are arranging baskets to receive cell phones before adjourning to the dining table, and an appreciative guest will gladly give theirs up before sitting down. Worried about missing a call from the babysitter? By all means, check your phone between courses if you must. Otherwise, you'll probably enjoy releasing the technology tether for a little while.

Tart Cherry
CRISP

Serves 6 to 8   *Hands-on 25 minutes*
Total 1 hour, 20 minutes

5 cups pitted fresh or frozen tart cherries, thawed, drained
1 cup granulated sugar
3 tablespoons cornstarch
½ teaspoon almond extract
9 tablespoons butter, softened
½ teaspoon salt
1 cup all-purpose flour
½ cup firmly packed brown sugar
¼ teaspoon ground cinnamon
¾ cup sliced almonds, coarsely chopped

1. Preheat oven to 350°F. Stir together first 3 ingredients in a medium-size nonaluminum saucepan; let stand 15 minutes or until juicy. Bring to a boil over medium heat, stirring constantly. Boil, whisking constantly, 1 minute or until thickened. Remove from heat; stir in almond extract, 1 tablepoon butter, and ¼ teaspoon salt. Pour mixture into a lightly greased 11- x 7-inch baking dish.

2. Stir together flour, brown sugar, cinnamon, and remaining ¼ teaspoon salt in a medium bowl. Using your hands, gently combine flour mixture, almonds, and remaining 8 tablespoons butter until mixture resembles small peas. Sprinkle over cherry mixture.

3. Bake at 350°F for 40 minutes or until filling is bubbly and topping is golden brown.

SUNDAYS PAST & PRESENT
with PATTI CALLAHAN HENRY

Meet Patti Callahan Henry, *New York Times* best-selling novelist.

HOMETOWN: A little bit of everywhere, USA **RESIDES:** Mountain Brook, AL

WHAT COMES TO MIND WHEN YOU THINK OF MEALS FROM SUNDAYS PAST?

My dad is a preacher, so I grew up going to church every Sunday and then coming home to the traditional Sunday lunch. Mom always prepared ahead of time. She'd set the table and the oven timer so that when we came home, the house smelled like pot roast or casserole, and like magic, she could put the rest of the meal on the table. We all ate together, and then we were free—naps, reading, or whatever the day wanted.

WHAT DISH DID YOU LOOK FORWARD TO HAVING?

Mashed potatoes. My mom would whip them up with the electric mixer and pour in all the good stuff—butter, salt, cream—and then whip them some more. To me, these potatoes were like meringue—sweet and buttery and healing.

TELL US ABOUT YOUR FAVORITE SUNDAY SUPPER—PAST OR PRESENT.

My favorite Sunday suppers were the ones during a holiday because they were the most elaborate. If I have to choose one, here it is: turkey, mashed potatoes, glazed carrots, cranberry sauce, and warm buttered biscuits.

This chicken-n-biscuit menu is easy to prepare and makes a great picnic supper. Fried, boneless, skinless chicken thighs nestled in a biscuit are just right for eating out of hand. The Zucchini-Potato Casserole is delicious warm or at room temperature, making it an ideal outdoor dish. The Garden Cocktail is a refreshing accompaniment.

Prepare the casserole in advance to allow the flavors to meld. The chicken can be fried and then chilled for the picnic or fried just before serving if eating at home. The base for the refreshing cocktail can be made up to one week ahead. Pack cocktail fixings separately.

CHICKEN *and Biscuits*

Serves 8   *Hands-on 40 minutes*   *Total 1 hour, 5 minutes*

FRIED CHICKEN THIGHS
8 skinned and boned chicken thighs
  (about 2¼ pounds)
1 teaspoon salt
½ teaspoon freshly ground black pepper
⅛ teaspoon onion powder
1 cup buttermilk
1 large egg
Vegetable oil
2 cups all-purpose flour

BISCUITS
2 cups bread flour
2 cups all-purpose flour
2 tablespoons baking powder
2 tablespoons sugar
1 teaspoon salt
1 cup butter, cut into small cubes
1½ cups buttermilk
1 large egg
Parchment paper
Toppings: Chopped pickled green tomatoes,
  local honey

1. Prepare Chicken: Sprinkle chicken thighs with salt and next 2 ingredients. Whisk together 1 cup buttermilk and 1 egg in a large bowl; add chicken, tossing to coat.

2. Pour oil to depth of 1 inch into a large cast-iron skillet; heat to 325°F. Place 2 cups flour in a shallow dish; dredge chicken in flour, shaking off excess. Fry chicken, in 2 batches, 5 to 6 minutes on each side or until golden brown and done. Drain on a wire rack over paper towels, and keep warm.

3. Prepare Biscuits: Combine bread flour and next 4 ingredients in a large bowl. Place cubed butter in a zip-top plastic freezer bag. Freeze flour mixture and butter separately 10 minutes or until well chilled. Whisk together 1½ cups buttermilk and 1 egg in a small bowl.

4. Cut chilled butter into flour mixture with a pastry blender or fork until crumbly. Add buttermilk mixture, stirring just until dry ingredients are moistened.

5. Preheat oven to 450°F. Turn dough out onto a lightly floured surface, and knead lightly 3 to 4 times. Pat or roll the dough to 1-inch thickness; cut into 8 squares, and place on a parchment paper–lined baking sheet.

6. Bake at 450°F for 15 to 16 minutes or until golden brown. Split biscuits; fill each with 1 cooked chicken thigh and desired toppings.

Garden
COCKTAIL

Serves 1   Hands-on 10 minutes
Total 3 hours, 15 minutes, including juice

1 tablespoon kosher salt
1 tablespoon finely chopped fresh flat-leaf parsley
1 lime wedge
½ medium tomato, seeded and chopped
1 fresh basil sprig
¼ cup gin
½ cup Garden Tomato Juice
Freshly ground black pepper
Garnishes: cucumber spears, celery ribs,
   fresh basil sprigs, lime wedges

Combine kosher salt and parsley. Rub rim of a glass with lime wedge;
dip rim in salt mixture to coat. Muddle tomato and basil sprig against
sides of glass to release flavors. Fill glass with ice. Stir in gin and
Garden Tomato Juice. Sprinkle with ground pepper, and garnish
with cucumber spears, celery ribs, fresh basil sprigs, or lime wedges,
if desired.

Garden Tomato Juice

Serves 8   Hands-on 10 minutes   Total 3 hours, 5 minutes

3 pounds very ripe red or yellow tomatoes, coarsely chopped
1¼ cups chopped celery with leaves
⅓ cup chopped onion
½ teaspoon kosher salt
½ teaspoon freshly ground black pepper

Bring tomatoes and remaining ingredients to a simmer in a large
nonaluminum saucepan over medium heat; simmer 25 minutes
or until vegetables are soft. Cool 30 minutes. Process, in 2 batches,
in a blender until smooth. Pour through a fine wire-mesh strainer
into a container, discarding solids. Cover and chill 2 hours.

Zucchini – Potato
CASSEROLE

Serves 6 to 8   *Hands-on 35 minutes*
Total 1 hour, 45 minutes

2 tablespoons butter
2 medium-size sweet onions, chopped
Vegetable cooking spray
1 medium-size Yukon gold potato, sliced
1 medium-size zucchini, sliced
4 plum tomatoes, sliced
1½ teaspoons kosher salt
¾ teaspoon freshly ground black pepper
2 tablespoons butter, melted
⅓ cup freshly grated Parmesan cheese

1. Preheat oven to 375°F. Melt 2 tablespoons butter in a medium skillet over medium heat; add onions, and sauté 10 to 12 minutes or until tender and onions begin to caramelize.

2. Spoon onions into a 10-inch quiche dish coated with cooking spray. Toss together potatoes and next 4 ingredients. Arrange potato, zucchini, and tomato slices in a single layer over onions, alternating and overlapping slightly. Drizzle with 2 tablespoons melted butter. Cover with aluminum foil.

3. Bake at 375°F for 30 minutes. Remove foil, and sprinkle with cheese. Bake 35 to 40 minutes or until golden brown. Let stand 10 minutes before serving.

MENU SIX

SERVES 4

This simple Sunday supper is an easy-to-prepare treat for kids and adults alike. Chunks of chicken breast are tossed in a robust spice mixture, then marinated in buttermilk to cool the palate. Coated with breadcrumbs and lightly fried, these chicken bites are a hit with everyone! Adjust the seasonings to suit your family's taste. A Summer Lime Fizz stems the heat, and for dessert, nothing makes you feel more like a kid than a tasty hand pie. Marinate the seasoned chicken bites in buttermilk early in the day, but cook them just before serving. The lime syrup for the fizz can be made up to a week ahead, but it should be done at least an hour before serving to leave time for chilling. The hand pies can be made up to two days in advance or served warm from the oven.

PICNIC CHICKEN BITES (page 41)

STRAWBERRY-RHUBARB HAND PIES (page 42)

SUMMER LIME FIZZ (page 44)

SET THE
SCENE

Grab a favorite wicker picnic basket and head outdoors with this easy take-along supper.

Spring brings us outdoors, and nothing celebrates the awakening like a picnic. These recipes are downsized and portable versions of some picnic classics: fried chicken and sweet pie. Sipping a tart and satisfying Summer Lime Fizz keeps things cool and refreshed.

Stave off hunger by starting with a fruit and cheese snack. No recipe needed to skewer blackberries, a mint leaf, and Bocconcino—the small pearls of mozzarella.

Round out the menu with a corn salsa, tossing fresh or frozen corn kernels into a favorite fresh salsa for a crunch twist. And don't forget the chips.

Stack up a load of vintage blankets to ward off any chill from the changeable temperatures of May, and add some festive retro linens. Grab a ball, a kite, and a long jump rope, and you are ready for outdoor family fun.

Picnic
CHICKEN BITES

Serves 4   Hands-on 50 minutes   Total 50 minutes, plus up to 12 hours for marinating

1½ teaspoons to 1 tablespoon ground red pepper
1½ teaspoons ground chipotle chile pepper
1½ teaspoons garlic powder
1½ teaspoons dried crushed red pepper
1½ teaspoons freshly ground black pepper
¾ teaspoon salt
½ teaspoon paprika
2 pounds skinned and boned chicken breasts
2 cups buttermilk
3 bread slices, toasted
1 cup all-purpose flour
Peanut oil
Blue cheese dressing or honey mustard

1. Combine first 7 ingredients in a small bowl; reserve half of spice mixture. Cut chicken into 1-inch pieces. Place chicken in a medium bowl, and toss with remaining spice mixture until coated. Stir in buttermilk; cover and chill up to 12 hours.

2. Tear bread into pieces, and place in a food processor with reserved spice mixture. Process until mixture resembles cornmeal. Stir in flour. Remove chicken pieces from buttermilk, discarding buttermilk. Dredge chicken in breadcrumb mixture.

3. Pour oil to depth of 2 inches into a Dutch oven; heat to 350°F. Fry chicken, in batches, 6 to 7 minutes on each side or until golden brown and done. Drain on a wire rack over paper towels. Sprinkle with salt to taste. Serve warm or cold with blue cheese dressing or honey mustard.

Strawberry – Rhubarb
HAND PIES

Makes 2 dozen   *Hands-on 1 hour*   *Total 1 hour, 40 minutes*

¾ cup finely diced fresh strawberries
¾ cup finely diced rhubarb
1 tablespoon cornstarch
6 tablespoons sugar
3 teaspoons orange zest
2 ¼ cups all-purpose flour
¼ teaspoon salt
½ cup butter, cold
¼ cup shortening, chilled
3 tablespoons ice-cold water
3 tablespoons orange juice
Parchment paper
1 egg yolk, beaten
1 tablespoon whipping cream
Sugar

1. Combine strawberries, rhubarb, cornstarch, 2 tablespoons sugar, and 1 ½ teaspoons orange zest in a small bowl.

2. Preheat oven to 375°F. Combine flour, salt, and remaining ¼ cup sugar in a large bowl. Cut in butter and shortening with a pastry blender until mixture resembles small peas. Stir in remaining 1 ½ teaspoons orange zest. Drizzle with 3 tablespoons ice-cold water and orange juice. Stir with a fork until combined. (Mixture will be crumbly and dry.) Knead mixture lightly, and shape dough into a disk. Divide dough in half.

3. Roll half of dough to ⅛-inch thickness on a heavily floured surface. (Cover remaining dough with plastic wrap.) Cut with a 2 ¼-inch round cutter, rerolling scraps as needed. Place half of dough rounds 2 inches apart on parchment paper–lined baking sheets. Top with 1 rounded teaspoonful strawberry mixture. Dampen edges of dough with water, and top with remaining dough rounds, pressing edges to seal. Crimp edges with a fork, and cut a slit in top of each round for steam to escape. Repeat procedure with remaining dough and strawberry mixture.

4. Stir together egg yolk and cream; brush pies with egg wash. Sprinkle with sugar. Freeze pies 10 minutes.

5. Bake at 375°F for 20 to 25 minutes or until lightly browned. Cool 10 minutes. Serve warm or at room temperature. Store in an airtight container up to 2 days.

Summer
LIME FIZZ

Makes 4³⁄₄ cups　　*Hands-on 5 minutes*
Total 1 hour, 15 minutes, including syrup

Crushed ice
¾ to 1 cup Lime Simple Syrup
½ cup fresh lime juice
3 ½ cups chilled club soda

Fill a large pitcher with crushed ice. Pour Lime Simple Syrup and lime juice over ice. Add club soda, and stir gently to combine. Serve immediately.

Lime Simple Syrup

Makes 1½ cups　　*Hands-on 10 minutes*
Total 1 hour, 10 minutes

1 cup sugar
1 tablespoon lime zest
½ cup fresh lime juice

Cook sugar and ½ cup water in a small saucepan over medium heat, stirring constantly, 3 minutes or until sugar is dissolved. Remove from heat; stir in lime zest and lime juice. Cover and chill 1 hour.

SOUTHERN SAVVY
INTRODUCTIONS

Once upon a time, introductions were very formal and followed strict rules. Today the environment is more relaxed, so there are just a few guidelines. In general, a younger person is introduced to an elder, a man to a woman, and individuals to someone holding a dignified status or office (such as a judge, member of the clergy, or elected official). Use first and last names wherever possible, such as "Catherine, I'd like you to meet Sam Smith. Sam, this is Catherine Jones." It's polite to stand when introduced and to respond "Pleased to meet you" or "How do you do?" A gracious host will also help facilitate a conversation starter, such as mentioning something the two have in common.

SUNDAYS PAST & PRESENT
with ERIKA COUNCIL

Meet Erika Council, Southern writer and photographer behind the food blog *Southern Soufflé*.
HOMETOWN: Raleigh, NC **RESIDES:** Atlanta, GA

WHAT COMES TO MIND WHEN YOU THINK OF MEALS FROM SUNDAYS PAST?

Biscuits, lots of them. My grandmother would make these amazing angel biscuits that would rise as we sat patiently in church. After church ended, I can still remember how eager I was for that warm basket of flaky buttered biscuits, as well as the crispy fried chicken that would often accompany them. Granny had a saying—"The chicken can bathe while the biscuits rise"—meaning her chicken sat in buttermilk while the biscuits would rise on the pan.

WHAT DISH DID YOU LOOK FORWARD TO HAVING?

Other than the usual fried chicken, I would definitely say those slow-roasted candied yams. They were always sweet and tender—an incredible addition to any meal.

TELL US ABOUT YOUR FAVORITE SUNDAY SUPPER—PAST OR PRESENT.

I've recently started hosting Sunday suppers about once a month. My favorite experience was when my normal dinner table of six turned into 16. Just seeing the array of people and the great energy that flowed around the dinner table reminded me of the past. Sunday dinner was when everyone gathered to celebrate the week and to relish in the company of loved ones and friends or sometimes complete strangers. The dinner table was a place where you could bring everything from your joys to your burdens and find comfort in food and good company. That particular day brought me back to those times.

En papillote is the French term meaning "in parchment," and fish baked and served *en papillote* is like having a present on your plate. No parchment? Aluminum foil is easily substituted for parchment to make the packets. Use our foolproof blanching method below and your veggies will look as good as they taste, making a colorful dish of bright-green vegetables, offset with the scarlet chowchow. Serve leftover chowchow with cheese and crackers, ham sandwiches, or burgers.

Your Sunday supper prep starts on Saturday with the meringues, which require a 12-hour drying time. But it's worth it for this take on a mud pie confection. The fish is best cooked just before serving. It's lovely to serve the parchment packets on individual plates so each diner has the pleasure of opening his or her own serving. A sharp knife or kitchen shears will do the trick. The aromatic steam is heaven. And don't forget to pass the basil. The vegetables can be blanched in advance and refrigerated. Sauté those in butter as directed while the fish is baking.

FISH IN PARCHMENT

Serves 4   *Hands-on 15 minutes*   *Total 30 minutes*

1 (8-ounce) package haricots verts
   (French green beans)
1 red bell pepper, thinly sliced
½ small red onion, thinly sliced
2 large tomatoes, chopped
2 tablespoons drained capers
⅓ cup green olives, quartered
Parchment paper
4 (4- to 5-ounce) fresh white fish fillets
   (such as snapper, triggerfish, flounder, or grouper)
1 teaspoon salt
½ teaspoon freshly ground black pepper
2 tablespoons olive oil
1 lemon, quartered
¼ cup torn fresh basil

1. Preheat oven to 400°F. Divide first 6 ingredients among 4 (17-inch) squares of parchment paper. Top each with 1 fish fillet. Sprinkle fish with salt and pepper; drizzle with olive oil. Squeeze juice from lemon over fish; place 1 lemon wedge on each fillet. Bring parchment paper sides up over mixture; double fold top and sides to seal, making packets. Place packets on a baking sheet.

2. Bake at 400°F for 15 to 20 minutes or until a thermometer registers 140° to 145°F when inserted through paper into fish. Place each packet on a plate, and cut open. Sprinkle fish with basil. Serve immediately.

Fennel-and-Potato
GRATIN

Serves 8   Hands-on 30 minutes   Total 1 hour, 22 minutes

3 tablespoons butter
1 shallot, sliced
1 garlic clove, minced
2 tablespoons all-purpose flour
1¼ cups half-and-half
½ (10 ounces) block sharp white Cheddar cheese, shredded
½ teaspoon salt
¼ teaspoon freshly ground black pepper
⅛ teaspoon ground nutmeg
2 large baking potatoes (about 2 pounds), peeled and thinly sliced
1 small fennel bulb, thinly sliced
Garnish: fresh rosemary leaves

1. Preheat oven to 400°F. Melt butter in a heavy saucepan over medium heat. Add shallot; sauté 2 to 3 minutes or until tender. Add the garlic, and sauté 1 minute.

2. Whisk in flour; cook, whisking constantly, 1 minute. Gradually whisk in the half-and-half; cook, whisking constantly, 3 to 4 minutes or until thickened and bubbly. Remove from heat. Whisk in Cheddar cheese until melted and smooth. Stir in salt and next 2 ingredients.

3. Layer potato and fennel slices alternately in a lightly greased, broiler-safe ceramic 2-quart casserole dish. Spread cheese sauce over layers. Cover with aluminum foil.

4. Bake at 400°F for 50 minutes or until potatoes are tender. Remove from oven. Increase oven temperature to broil with oven rack 5 inches from heat. Uncover dish, and broil 2 to 4 minutes or until golden brown. Garnish with rosemary.

Mud Pie Meringue
SUNDAES

Serves 6   *Hands-on 20 minutes*   *Total 13 hours, 50 minutes*

Parchment paper
3 large egg whites (at room temperature)
½ teaspoon vanilla extract
⅛ teaspoon cream of tartar
½ cup sugar
2 tablespoons sifted unsweetened cocoa
2 cups coffee ice cream
4 cream-filled chocolate sandwich cookies, crushed
2 tablespoons chopped toasted pecans
3 tablespoons chocolate sundae syrup

1. Preheat oven to 225°F. Cover a large baking sheet with parchment paper. Draw 6 (3-inch) circles on paper. Turn paper over; secure with masking tape.

2. Place egg whites, vanilla, and cream of tartar in a large bowl; beat at high speed with an electric mixer until foamy. Gradually add sugar, 1 tablespoon at a time, beating mixture until stiff peaks form. Gently fold in cocoa.

3. Divide egg white mixture evenly among the 6 drawn circles. Shape meringues into nests with 1-inch sides, using the back of a spoon.

4. Bake at 225°F for 1½ hours or until dry. Turn oven off, and cool meringues in closed oven at least 12 hours. Remove from oven; carefully remove meringues from paper.

5. Place meringues on individual dessert plates. Top each with ⅓ cup ice cream. Sprinkle each evenly with 1½ tablespoons cookie crumbs and 1 teaspoon pecans; drizzle each with 1½ teaspoons chocolate syrup. Serve immediately.

This Sunday supper couldn't be easier—or more flavorful. Tomatoes, shrimp, roasted red peppers, and feta cheese combine to create a subtly salty, succulent dish. The salad is a just-right mix of herbs and greens. And who doesn't love a shortbread-based cookie bar (with extras to tuck inside Monday's school lunch)?

Prepare the shortbread bars early in the day or even a day in advance for this menu. The shrimp dish is a quick-prep and quick-cook one that is perfect for a busy Sunday filled with ball games, recitals, or lessons. Jarred roasted red peppers are a pantry staple for me and add so much flavor to nearly any dish you can think of. The bread cubes really make this salad special—and attractive to the salad naysayers. Olive bread is particularly wonderful, but use whatever you have on hand, especially if it is a fancy, flavorful one.

Tomato and Feta
SHRIMP

Serves 6   *Hands-on 10 minutes*   *Total 35 minutes*

2 pints grape tomatoes
3 garlic cloves, sliced
3 tablespoons olive oil
1 teaspoon kosher salt
½ teaspoon freshly ground black pepper
1½ pounds peeled and deveined, medium-size raw shrimp
½ cup chopped jarred roasted red bell peppers
½ cup chopped fresh parsley
1 (4-ounce) package crumbled feta cheese
2 tablespoons fresh lemon juice
Crusty French bread, sliced

Preheat oven to 450°F. Place tomatoes and next 4 ingredients in a 13- x 9-inch baking dish, tossing gently to coat. Bake for 15 minutes. Stir in shrimp and peppers. Bake for 10 to 15 minutes or just until shrimp turn pink. Toss with parsley, feta cheese, and lemon juice. Serve immediately with crusty French bread.

Herbs and Greens
SALAD

Serves 6 to 8   *Hands-on 10 minutes*   *Total 30 minutes*

½ teaspoon lemon zest
4 tablespoons olive oil
3 cups (1-inch) olive bread cubes
4 cups torn butter lettuce (about 1 head)
2 cups firmly packed fresh baby spinach
1 cup torn escarole
½ cup loosely packed fresh parsley leaves
¼ cup fresh (1-inch) chive pieces
2 tablespoons fresh lemon juice

1. Preheat oven to 425°F. Stir together lemon zest and 1 tablespoon olive oil in a large bowl. Add bread cubes, and toss to coat. Arrange in a single layer on a baking sheet. Bake for 5 minutes or until crisp. Let cool completely (about 15 minutes).

2. Meanwhile, combine butter lettuce and next 4 ingredients in a large bowl. Drizzle with lemon juice and remaining 3 tablespoons olive oil, and toss to coat. Add salt and pepper to taste. Serve immediately with toasted bread cubes.

Ciabatta, focaccia, or country white bread may be substituted for olive bread.

Peach Melba
SHORTBREAD BARS

Makes 1½ to 2 dozen bars   *Hands-on 20 minutes*
Total 2 hours, 20 minutes

2 cups all-purpose flour
½ cup granulated sugar
¼ teaspoon salt
1 cup cold butter
1 cup peach preserves
6 teaspoons raspberry preserves
½ cup sliced almonds

1. Preheat oven to 350°F. Combine first 3 ingredients in a medium bowl. Cut in butter with a pastry blender until crumbly. Reserve 1 cup flour mixture.

2. Lightly grease an 11- x 7-inch or 9-inch square pan. Press remaining flour mixture onto bottom of prepared pan.

3. Bake at 350°F for 25 to 30 minutes or until lightly browned.

4. Spread peach preserves over crust in pan. Dollop raspberry preserves by ½ teaspoonfuls over peach preserves. Sprinkle reserved 1 cup flour mixture over preserves. Sprinkle with almonds.

5. Bake at 350°F for 35 to 40 minutes or until golden brown. Let cool 1 hour on a wire rack. Cut into bars.

MENU NINE

SERVES 6

A Sunday roast chicken is nearly everyone's favorite, and this recipe couldn't be easier. The olive oil helps to brown and crisp the skin, and the rosemary and lemon give the birds fabulous flavor and a seductive aroma. Get a jumpstart on your week by roasting two, yielding extra meat for use during the week. Browned and caramelized roasted vegetables are cozy companions for the chicken. Never made your own marshmallows? This is the recipe to try. The bouncy, spongy texture is just as it should be, and the taste is far better than the store-bought variety. Plan ahead to prepare the marshmallows, allowing for the three hours of drying time. Allow two hours for preparing and baking the chickens—they are tastiest served just after the resting time. Prepare the vegetables early in the day. Refrigerate and reheat in a skillet while the chicken is resting.

CLASSIC
ROAST CHICKENS (page 57)

ROASTED CARROTS,
TURNIP ROOTS, AND
VIDALIA ONIONS (page 58)

HOMEMADE
MARSHMALLOWS (page 60)

SCENE

Roast chicken has become a staple in our menus, but not too long ago it was considered a very special meal, worthy of presenting to a guest or the preacher at the Sunday table.

Chickens were expensive, mostly due to the short supply. If one kept chickens in the yard, they were for their precious eggs. Once a laying hen was finished with her duties, she indeed would be a "tough old bird" and only fit for stewing. Fresh chicken was available at the market, but the price was high. Once the South became industrialized and factory farms were established, fresh chicken became widely available and more affordable.

A classic roast chicken can cure what ails us. After a long bout of the flu as a child, I couldn't wait to have a real dinner. My request was roast chicken, mashed potatoes, and green beans. I can still remember the taste of that meal. And who hasn't experienced the curative power of homemade chicken soup?

Even in the fanciest of restaurants you'll see roast chicken on the menu. It is the mark of a great cook who can produce a flavorful and moist chicken from the oven. Now you can, too.

Classic
ROAST CHICKENS

Makes 2 chickens　　　*Hands-on 20 minutes*　　　*Total 2 hours*

4 teaspoons kosher salt
2 teaspoons freshly ground black pepper
2 (4- to 5-pound) whole chickens
2 lemons, halved
2 fresh rosemary sprigs
1 tablespoon olive oil
Vegetable cooking spray

1. Preheat oven to 375°F. Stir together salt and pepper. If applicable, remove necks and giblets from chickens, and reserve for another use. Pat chickens dry.

2. Sprinkle ½ teaspoon salt mixture inside cavity of each chicken. Place 2 lemon halves and 1 rosemary sprig inside cavity of each chicken. Rub 1½ teaspoons olive oil into skin of each chicken. Sprinkle with remaining salt mixture; rub into skin. Tuck chicken wings under, if desired. Lightly grease a wire rack in a 17- x 12-inch jelly-roll pan with cooking spray. Place chickens, breast sides up and facing in opposite directions (for even browning), on wire rack.

3. Bake at 375°F for 1½ hours or until a meat thermometer inserted in thigh registers 180°F. Cover and let stand 10 minutes before slicing.

4. Remove meat from the bones of the second chicken and allow to cool. Store 2 days in airtight containers in the refrigerator or up to 2 months in the freezer.

Resist the temptation to carve the chicken right away. Resting the chicken on the cutting board for at least 10 minutes after roasting allows the juices to redistribute into the meat, making it moist and tender.

Roasted Carrots, Turnip Roots, and
VIDALIA ONIONS

Serves 6　　　*Hands-on 20 minutes*　　　*Total 1 hour, 15 minutes*

2 pounds carrots
1 pound turnip roots, cut into 1½-inch pieces
　(about 3 medium-size turnip roots)
1 pound Vidalia onions, cut into 1½-inch pieces
　(about 1 large onion)
¼ cup extra-virgin olive oil
1 teaspoon salt
½ teaspoon freshly ground pepper

1. Preheat oven to 450°F. Cut carrots in half lengthwise, and, if they are large, into 4-inch pieces. Arrange carrots, turnip roots, and onions on 2 jelly-roll pans.

2. Toss vegetables with olive oil, and sprinkle with salt and pepper.

3. Bake at 450°F for 55 minutes or until tender and beginning to brown, stirring vegetables and rotating pans once halfway through baking.

SOUTHERN SAVVY
TARDY

There is rarely an acceptable excuse for a guest to be late. Weddings are seldom interrupted to allow late guests to be seated, and theater performances shutter their doors until a suitable break or intermission. Being late is a sign that a guest has not taken the host's time or effort seriously. Certainly things can happen to get off schedule, the most common being bad traffic, and contacting your host as soon as possible is the polite course. If you anticipate being more than 15 minutes late, insist that your host begin without you. It is your host's option to decide whether or not to wait. Upon arrival, join in immediately; a gracious host will introduce you, and the event will continue. This is the one occasion where guests need not rise to meet the late arrival.

Homemade
MARSHMALLOWS

Makes 2 dozen   Hands-on 35 minutes
Total 45 minutes, plus 3 hours for drying

Wax paper
1 cup powdered sugar
½ cup cornstarch
3 envelopes unflavored gelatin (about 3 tablespoons)
3 cups granulated sugar
1 cup light corn syrup
¼ teaspoon salt
2 teaspoons vanilla extract

1. Line a 13- x 9-inch baking pan with wax paper. Combine powdered sugar and ½ cup cornstarch in a bowl. Sift about ½ sugar-cornstarch mixture over wax paper; set remaining mixture aside.

2. Combine gelatin and ½ cup water in bowl of a heavy-duty electric stand mixer; let stand 10 minutes.

3. Combine granulated sugar, corn syrup, salt, and ½ cup water in a large saucepan. Bring to a boil over medium-high heat; boil for 1 minute.

4. Turn mixer on low speed; add vanilla to gelatin mixture. Carefully, add hot sugar mixture in a slow steady stream. Increase speed to high; beat for 10 minutes or until thick. Spread mixture evenly into prepared pan. Sift ½ cup powdered sugar mixture over mixture in pan.

5. Spread marshmallow mixture evenly in pan. Let stand for 3 to 4 hours.

6. Turn out onto wax paper. Cut into desired shapes. Toss marshmallows with remaining reserved powdered sugar mixture in bowl. Store in airtight containers.

Make the marshmallows even more fun using different shaped cutters.

SUNDAYS PAST & PRESENT
with NATHALIE DUPREE

Meet Nathalie Dupree, cookbook writer and television host.

RESIDES: Charleston, SC

WHAT COMES TO MIND WHEN YOU THINK OF MEALS FROM SUNDAYS PAST?

Ma Ma Dupree's house in Augusta, Georgia, and her Sunday dinner in the middle of the day. She would fill the table with garden-fresh vegetables, as well as piping hot fried chicken or another meat.

WHAT DISH DID YOU LOOK FORWARD TO HAVING?

Ma Ma had a number of specialties, but among my favorites were her creamed corn and her caramel cake. We tried to get that recipe from her but never could get it exactly. Dessert was always served in the living room (she called it the parlor) except ice cream, which was sometimes served outside on the porch.

TELL US ABOUT YOUR FAVORITE SUNDAY SUPPER—PAST OR PRESENT.

After dinner, Ma Ma would spread a clean white tablecloth, perhaps with a few darned places, over the food in the bowls and platters left on the table. This would keep flying creatures away, as well as little hands that might knock over a bowl of butter beans. For supper, she would unveil the table, adding more fresh tomato or melon slices, and we would finish off the food, every bit as good at room temperature as it was when it sizzled.

Sunday supper to me is always a casual affair, after a big dinner at midday. I frequently serve tasty leftovers or vegetables. Sometimes it is grilled cheese or other sandwiches. I don't worry about having meat—or even a balanced meal. We've already eaten enough to get our vitamins, so it is just to give us another chance to visit and catch up on the week's events.

MENU TEN

SERVES 8

ONE-POT SHRIMP AND GRITS (PAGE 63)

HEIRLOOM TOMATO SALAD WITH LADY PEA SALSA (PAGE 64)

SUMPTUOUS SWOON PIES
(PAGE 65)

The South Carolina Lowcountry, the birthplace of shrimp and grits, boasts almost as many versions of this dish as there are days in the year. Spicy andouille, sautéed shrimp, and creamy grits are the backbone of flavor for this One-Pot Shrimp and Grits. Avoid overcrowding the pot when cooking the shrimp so they will brown and cook through quickly. Celebrate the season with the best summer tomatoes available, topped with delicate Southern lady peas in a fresh salsa with nectarine, jalapeño, ginger, cilantro, and red onion. The salsa also makes a great topping for grilled meats, fish, or chicken. Swoon Pies are our take on the iconic marshmallow-filled pastry known around the South. This one has tender graham cookies dipped in chocolate and a few special toppings.

Prepare the pies in advance to allow for the cooling and freezing times. The salsa can be made up to a day ahead. The shrimp and grits are best prepared just before serving.

One-Pot SHRIMP AND GRITS

Serves 8   Hands-on 35 minutes   Total 1 hour, 5 minutes

8 ounces andouille sausage, diced
3 tablespoons olive oil
1 ¼ pounds peeled, large raw shrimp, deveined
1 medium-size sweet onion, chopped
2 celery ribs, chopped
3 garlic cloves, sliced
1 cup dry white wine
6 cups vegetable broth
1 (14 ½-ounce) can fire-roasted diced tomatoes, drained
½ green bell pepper, diced
½ red bell pepper, diced
½ cup chopped green onions
1 ½ teaspoons Cajun seasoning
1 teaspoon kosher salt
½ teaspoon freshly ground black pepper
1 ½ cups uncooked regular grits
2 tablespoons chopped fresh oregano

1. Cook sausage in a large Dutch oven over medium heat, stirring often, 5 to 7 minutes or until browned. Remove sausage using a slotted spoon; reserve drippings in Dutch oven. Drain sausage on paper towels.

2. Stir oil into drippings. Cook shrimp, in batches, in hot drippings over medium-high heat 1 to 2 minutes on each side or until opaque; remove with slotted spoon. Reduce heat to medium.

3. Sauté onion and celery in Dutch oven over medium heat 3 to 5 minutes or until tender. Add garlic, and sauté 1 minute. Stir in wine, and cook, stirring occasionally, 5 minutes or until reduced by half. Stir in broth and next 7 ingredients, and bring to a boil over medium-high heat. Whisk in grits; return mixture to a boil, whisking constantly. Reduce heat to medium-low; simmer, stirring occasionally, 20 to 25 minutes or until thickened. Stir in oregano, reserved sausage, and shrimp. Cook, stirring occasionally, 5 more minutes.

Heirloom Tomato
SALAD
with Lady Pea Salsa

Serves 8   Hands-on 15 minutes
Total 50 minutes, including salsa

4 pounds assorted heirloom tomatoes
2 small Kirby cucumbers, sliced
1 small red onion, halved and sliced
Lady Pea Salsa
Fresh basil leaves

Cut tomatoes into wedges or in half, depending on size. Gently toss tomatoes with cucumber and onion slices. Top with Lady Pea Salsa and basil.

Lady Pea Salsa

Makes about 4 cups   Hands-on 20 minutes
Total 35 minutes

1 cup diced unpeeled nectarine
2 jalapeño peppers, seeded and minced
1 tablespoon sugar
3 tablespoons fresh lime juice
2 teaspoons orange zest
2 teaspoons grated fresh ginger
2 cups cooked fresh lady peas
½ cup chopped fresh cilantro
⅓ cup diced red onion

Stir together first 6 ingredients in a large bowl; let stand 15 minutes. Add peas and next 2 ingredients, and gently toss to coat. Serve immediately, or refrigerate in an airtight container up to 24 hours.

Sumptuous
SWOON PIES

Makes 12 pies   Hands-on 45 minutes
Total 2 hours, 28 minutes, including filling

1 cup all-purpose flour
½ teaspoon baking powder
½ teaspoon baking soda
½ teaspoon salt
1 cup graham cracker crumbs
½ cup butter, softened
½ cup granulated sugar
½ cup firmly packed light brown sugar
1 large egg
1 teaspoon vanilla extract
1 (8-ounce) container sour cream
Parchment paper
Marshmallow Filling
1 (12-ounce) package semisweet chocolate morsels
2 teaspoons shortening
Toppings: chopped roasted salted pecans, chopped crystallized ginger, sea salt

1. Preheat oven to 350°F. Sift together flour and next 3 ingredients in a medium bowl; stir in graham cracker crumbs.

2. Beat butter and next 2 ingredients at medium speed with a heavy-duty electric stand mixer until fluffy. Add egg and vanilla, beating until blended. Add flour mixture to butter mixture alternately with sour cream, beginning and ending with flour mixture. Beat at low speed until blended after each addition, stopping to scrape down sides as needed.

3. Drop batter by rounded tablespoonfuls 2 inches apart onto 2 parchment paper-lined baking sheets. Bake, in batches, at 350°F for 13 to 15 minutes or until set and bottoms are golden brown. Remove cookies (on parchment paper) to wire racks, and cool completely (about 30 minutes).

4. Turn 12 cookies over, bottom sides up. Spread each with 1 heaping tablespoonful Marshmallow Filling. Top with remaining 12 cookies, bottom sides down, and press gently to spread filling to edges. Freeze on a parchment paper-lined baking sheet 30 minutes or until filling is set.

5. Place chocolate and shortening in a 2-cup glass measuring cup. Microwave at HIGH for 1 to 2 minutes, stirring every 30 seconds, until melted and smooth. Meanwhile, remove cookies from freezer, and let stand 10 minutes. Dip half of each cookie sandwich into melted chocolate mixture. Place on parchment paper-lined baking sheet. Sprinkle with desired toppings, and freeze 10 minutes or until chocolate is set.

Marshmallow Filling

Beat ½ cup softened butter at medium speed with an electric mixer until creamy; gradually add 1 cup powdered sugar, beating well. Add 1 cup marshmallow crème and ½ teaspoon vanilla extract, beating until well blended. Makes about 1½ cups.

MENU ELEVEN

SERVES 6

SLOW-COOKER
PORK (PAGE 67)

BAKED MACARONI
AND CHEESE (PAGE 68)

WHITE CHOCOLATE
CHIP OATMEAL
COOKIES (PAGE 69)

Sunday afternoon sports—whether it's a family game in the yard or a television matchup—call for an easy-prep meal, and nothing beats the convenience of a slow cooker. A workhorse in the kitchen, the slow cooker leaves you plenty of time to enjoy the game. This succulent pork shoulder roast cooks in a combination of barbecue sauce and cola soft drink, yielding a moist, fork-tender roast. Be adventurous and try other dark sodas such as root beer or cherry cola for a slightly different flavor. The macaroni and cheese is a cozy side dish for the heavenly pork. The variations are endless, so you can create your own family favorite. And who will resist a homemade cookie?

Your mealtime strategy for this menu can be as easy as you like as all three of these recipes can be made ahead. The pork should be put on to cook in mid-morning, unless cooked ahead, frozen, and reheated for serving. The macaroni and cheese can be assembled early, minus the topping, and refrigerated until ready to bake for supper. The cookies are a kid-friendly kitchen activity, so slot that recipe into your day depending on if you'd like kitchen helpers. The cookies can even be made ahead and frozen, then put out to defrost shortly before supper.

Slow–Cooker
PORK

Serves 6   Hands-on 5 minutes   Total 8 hours, 5 minutes

1 (4- to 5-pound) boneless pork shoulder roast
  (Boston butt), trimmed
1 (18-ounce) bottle barbecue sauce
1 (12-ounce) can cola soft drink

1. Place roast in a lightly greased 6-quart slow cooker; pour barbecue sauce and cola over roast. Cover and cook on LOW 8 to 10 hours or until meat shreds easily with a fork.

2. Transfer pork to a cutting board; shred with two forks, removing any large pieces of fat. Skim fat from sauce, and stir in shredded pork.

Baked
MACARONI
AND CHEESE

Serves 8   Hands-on 25 minutes   Total 1 hour

1 pound uncooked cellentani (corkscrew) pasta
2 tablespoons butter
¼ cup all-purpose flour
3 cups milk
1 (12-ounce) can evaporated milk
1 cup (4 ounces) shredded smoked Gouda cheese
½ cup (2 ounces) shredded sharp Cheddar cheese
3 ounces cream cheese, softened
½ teaspoon salt
¼ teaspoon ground red pepper
1¼ cups cornflakes cereal, crushed
1 tablespoon butter, melted

1. Preheat oven to 350°F. Prepare cellentani pasta according to package directions.

2. Meanwhile, melt 2 tablespoons butter in a Dutch oven over medium heat. Gradually whisk in flour; cook, whisking constantly, 1 minute. Gradually whisk in milk and evaporated milk until smooth; cook, whisking constantly, 8 to 10 minutes or until slightly thickened. Whisk in Gouda cheese, next 3 ingredients, and ⅛ teaspoon ground red pepper until smooth. Remove from heat, and stir in pasta.

3. Pour pasta mixture into a lightly greased 13- x 9-inch baking dish. Stir together crushed cereal, 1 tablespoon melted butter, and remaining ⅛ teaspoon ground red pepper; sprinkle over pasta mixture.

4. Bake at 350°F for 30 minutes or until golden and bubbly. Let stand 5 minutes before serving.

White Chocolate Chip
OATMEAL COOKIES

Makes about 5 dozen   **Hands-on 20 minutes**
Total 35 minutes

1 cup butter, softened
1 cup firmly packed light brown sugar
1 cup granulated sugar
2 large eggs
2 teaspoons vanilla extract
3 cups all-purpose flour
1 teaspoon baking soda
1 teaspoon baking powder
1 teaspoon salt
1½ cups uncooked regular oats
2 cups (12 ounces) white chocolate morsels
1 cup coarsely chopped pecans

1. Preheat oven to 350°F. Beat butter at medium speed with an electric mixer until creamy; gradually add sugars, beating well. Add eggs, one at a time, beating just until yellow disappears after each addition. Stir in vanilla.

2. Combine flour and next 3 ingredients; gradually add to butter mixture, beating until blended. Stir in oats, morsels, and pecans. Drop by tablespoonfuls onto greased baking sheets.

3. Bake at 350°F for 12 minutes. Cool on baking sheets 5 minutes; remove to wire racks to cool completely.

Bake cookies on shiny, heavy aluminum baking sheets. These sheets with no sides are designed for easily sliding cookies onto a cooling rack. Cool cookies completely before storing them in airtight containers.

Chapter 2
GREAT GRILLING

In the South, grilling is practically a year-round sport. And whether you choose to dine outside or in, the taste of supper cooked on the grill is hard to beat. Grilling over charcoal or with gas, on direct or indirect heat, using wood chips or planks, or in a bona fide smoker, the great outdoors soaks into every slightly charred bite.

The domain of the backyard grill has long been under the direction of the men in the family, but that's changing now. I enjoyed moist, juicy hamburgers on the grill hundreds of nights when I was growing up and was taught how to stuff and light a charcoal chimney starter. I now commandeer a gas grill, but I wish my grandfather were still here to cook the burgers.

These recipes will entice you to get fired up and cook outside, from juicy *Spice-Rubbed Rib-eye Steaks, Grilled Spicy Chicken,* and *Barbecue Kabobs* to *Lemon Grilled Salmon, Shrimp and Vegetable Rice,* and *Grilled Sausages with Asparagus,* and last but not least, *Smoky Ribs.* And all the sides are overflowing with fresh vegetables—*Jicama-and-Bell Pepper Slaw, Watermelon and Fennel Salad, Strawberry-Tomato Salad,* and more.

Grilling is a casual affair, so no need to get fancy. My must-haves? Plenty of cold beverages and lots of napkins.

MENU ONE
SERVES 8

GRILLED STEAK AND SALAD (PAGE 73)

OKRA AND TOMATOES (PAGE 74)

PRALINE KEY LIME PIE (PAGE 75)

Quick-grilling steaks require only about five to seven minutes of grill time per side, making this supper a summer favorite. Sautéed onion and walnuts enliven the mustard vinaigrette for the finished salad. Cooking quickly in a skillet, the okra side dish doesn't develop the slimy quality known to its detractors. The chilled, creamy Key lime pie is the dessert equivalent of a swimming hole—so refreshing you can't help but dive in. It's extra special with the addition of pecans in the crust as well as pecans and caramel at the bottom of the pie. Prepare the pie early in the day to allow for the cooking and chilling time (about five hours total). Prepare the okra and tomatoes while the steaks are grilling, or sauté before grilling steaks, and leave at room temperature until serving.

Grilled
STEAK AND SALAD

Serves 8   *Hands-on 20 minutes*   *Total 30 minutes*

1 small red onion, thinly sliced
½ cup olive oil
1 cup coarsely chopped walnuts
1 garlic clove, thinly sliced
2 pounds flat-iron, hanger, or tri-tip steak
2 tablespoons olive oil
1 tablespoon Chicago steak seasoning
1 teaspoon kosher salt
2 large red onions, cut into ½-inch-thick slices
⅓ cup white wine vinegar
1 tablespoon dark brown sugar
1 tablespoon whole grain Dijon mustard
¼ teaspoon freshly ground black pepper
1 romaine lettuce heart, torn
2 ounces crumbled blue cheese

1. Preheat grill to 350° to 400°F (medium-high) heat. Sauté thinly sliced small onion in ½ cup hot olive oil in a large skillet over medium-high heat 3 to 4 minutes or until golden and tender. Add walnuts and garlic; cook, stirring occasionally, 3 to 4 minutes or until walnuts just begin to turn golden brown. Remove from heat, and cool 5 minutes.

2. Rub steak with 1 tablespoon olive oil, steak seasoning, and ½ teaspoon salt. Toss ½-inch onion slices with remaining 1 tablespoon olive oil.

3. Grill steak, covered with grill lid, 5 to 7 minutes on each side or to desired degree of doneness. At the same time, grill thick onion slices, covered with grill lid, 4 to 5 minutes on each side or until golden brown. Remove steak and onions from grill, and let stand 5 minutes. Thinly slice steak.

4. Whisk together vinegar, brown sugar, and mustard in a medium bowl. Gradually whisk in walnut mixture. Add ¼ teaspoon pepper and remaining ½ teaspoon salt.

5. Toss lettuce and grilled onions with ¼ cup vinaigrette in a large bowl; arrange on a serving platter. Top with grilled steak. Sprinkle with crumbled blue cheese. Serve with remaining ¼ cup vinaigrette.

Okra and
TOMATOES

Serves 8   *Hands-on 15 minutes*   *Total 15 minutes*

1 pound fresh okra
1 large shallot
3 tablespoons olive oil
2 large green tomatoes, chopped
1 quart grape tomatoes, halved
3 garlic cloves, minced
½ cup torn fresh basil leaves
½ cup fresh flat-leaf parsley leaves
½ teaspoon salt
½ teaspoon freshly ground black pepper

1. Slice okra into ½-inch pieces and thinly slice shallot; sauté in 2 tablespoons of hot olive oil in a large skillet over medium-high heat 6 to 8 minutes or until okra is golden brown; transfer to a bowl.

2. Heat 1 tablespoon olive oil in skillet. Add green tomato, grape tomatoes, and garlic. Cook, stirring often, 2 minutes or until softened.

3. Combine tomatoes and okra mixture. Stir in basil, parsley, salt, and freshly ground black pepper.

Praline
KEY LIME PIE

Serves 8   *Hands-on 30 minutes*   *Total 6 hours, 53 minutes*

1 ¼ cups chopped pecans
2 cups graham cracker crumbs
½ cup butter, melted
¼ cup firmly packed light brown sugar
½ cup plus 2 tablespoons jarred caramel topping
2 (14-ounce) cans sweetened condensed milk
6 egg yolks
2 teaspoons Key lime or lime zest
1 cup fresh Key lime or lime juice
1 ½ cups whipping cream
¼ cup plus 2 tablespoons powdered sugar
2 sliced limes, plus lime zest curls, optional

1. Preheat oven to 350°F. Bake pecans in a single layer in a shallow pan 8 to 10 minutes or until toasted and fragrant, stirring halfway through.

2. Stir together graham cracker crumbs, next 2 ingredients, and ½ cup toasted pecans until blended. Press crumb mixture on bottom, up sides, and onto lip of a lightly greased 10-inch deep-dish pie plate.

3. Bake at 350°F for 10 to 12 minutes or until lightly browned. Remove from oven to a wire rack, and cool completely (about 45 minutes).

4. Sprinkle remaining ¾ cup toasted pecans over bottom of crust; drizzle caramel topping over pecans.

5. Whisk together sweetened condensed milk and next 3 ingredients. Gently pour into prepared crust.

6. Bake at 350°F for 20 to 25 minutes or until almost set. (The center will not be firm but will set up as it chills.) Cool completely on a wire rack (about 1 hour). Cover and chill 4 hours.

7. Beat whipping cream at high speed with an electric mixer until foamy; gradually add powdered sugar, beating until soft peaks form. Dollop or spread over pie.

8. Garnish with optional lime slices and curls.

To make squeezing fresh lime juice easy, remove limes from the refrigerator up to an hour before you plan to squeeze them. Then, roll them a few times on the counter to loosen the juices.

MENU TWO

SERVES 6

Rib-eye steaks are among the most flavorful and tender. They are well suited to grilling and cook relatively quickly—about 8 minutes per side. This herb-and-spice mixture adds tremendous flavor to the slightly charred exterior of the steak. The Fried Confetti Corn is topped with crunchy bacon and sautéed with red and green peppers.

Glazed pecan pieces add a streusel-like crunch to the tops of these Blackberry-Peach Cobbler Bars, and the recipe might leave you with one or two for your morning coffee the next day.

Let the steaks marinate for an hour in the refrigerator before grilling. Plan to make the cobbler bars early in the day, as they need to be fully cooled before cutting. The corn dish is best made just before serving.

SPICE-RUBBED RIB-EYE STEAKS (page 78)

FRIED CONFETTI CORN (page 81)

BLACKBERRY-PEACH COBBLER BARS (page 82)

SCENE

Traditions are what create memories, and the family table is at the heart of many traditions that will be remembered, and carried on, far into the future.

For our family, dining by candlelight has been a steadfast tradition. It began as a holdover from our dating and newly married life. By the time we became parents, it was a habit. I think it brought a calmness to the house—a serene scene that even our newborn sensed.

Every now and then I would save a few candles when they had burned down with just a couple of inches remaining. I'd toss them into a zip-top bag and tote them along on vacation. As we often rented a house or apartment when we traveled, I had our candles at the ready. The candles also provided an instant craft project for the kids—finding shells, or stones, or sticks—that could be turned into bases for the candles.

Our children's friends always felt special when they shared supper with us, as dining by candlelight seemed so grown-up. I think it helped everyone linger just a little longer at the table. My children have now left home, but they have taken this tradition with them.

Spice-Rubbed
RIB-EYE STEAKS

Serves 6   *Hands-on 15 minutes*   *Total 1 hour, 31 minutes*

2 ½ teaspoons freshly ground black pepper
1 tablespoon dried thyme
1 ½ teaspoons salt
4 ½ teaspoons garlic powder
1 ½ teaspoons lemon pepper
1 ½ teaspoons ground red pepper
1 ½ teaspoons dried parsley flakes
6 (1 ½-inch-thick) rib-eye steaks
3 tablespoons olive oil

1. Combine first 7 ingredients. Brush steaks with oil; rub with pepper mixture. Cover and chill 1 hour.

2. Preheat grill to medium-high (350° to 400°F) heat. Grill, covered with grill lid, 8 to 10 minutes on each side or to desired degree of doneness.

To prevent food from sticking, lightly coat the grate with an oil that has a high smoke point before turning on the grill. Peanut oil is a good choice. Cooking spray works, too.

Fried
CONFETTI CORN

Serves 8   Hands-on 30 minutes   Total 30 minutes

8 bacon slices
6 cups fresh sweet corn kernels (about 8 ears)
1 cup diced sweet onion
½ cup chopped red bell pepper
½ cup chopped green bell pepper
1 (8-ounce) package cream cheese, cubed
½ cup half-and-half
1 teaspoon sugar
1 teaspoon salt
1 teaspoon freshly ground black pepper

1. Cook bacon in a large skillet over medium-high heat 6 to 8 minutes or until crisp. Remove bacon, and drain on paper towels, reserving 2 tablespoons drippings in skillet. Coarsely crumble bacon.

2. Sauté corn and next 3 ingredients in hot drippings in skillet over medium-high heat 6 minutes or until tender. Add cream cheese and half-and-half, stirring until cream cheese melts. Stir in sugar and next 2 ingredients. Transfer to a serving dish, and top with bacon.

SOUTHERN SAVVY
THE RSVP

Lamentable is the state of the RSVP. All politeness seems to have vanished around the proper response to an invitation. The rules may have relaxed, but a host still needs to know if you plan to attend. Hosts who have issued invitations with "regrets only" mean for you to respond only if you cannot attend. Otherwise they are to assume that you are attending. If just RSVP appears, you are to let the host know of your intention either way. Last-minute cancellations, for whatever reason, are to be avoided if at all possible and are to be given to the host by phone as soon as possible.

Blackberry–Peach
COBBLER BARS

Serves 10 to 12   Hands-on 20 minutes
Total 2 hours, 20 minutes

1 cup butter, softened
1 cup firmly packed light brown sugar
1½ cups granulated sugar
4 large eggs
1 tablespoon vanilla extract
1 teaspoon baking powder
¾ teaspoon salt
3¼ cups all-purpose flour
3 (6-ounce) packages fresh blackberries (about 4 cups)
4 cups peeled and sliced fresh firm, ripe peaches
3 tablespoons bourbon
1 cup roasted glazed pecan pieces

1. Preheat oven to 350°F. Beat first 2 ingredients and 1 cup granulated sugar at medium speed with an electric mixer until creamy. Add eggs, 1 at a time, beating just until blended after each addition. Stir in vanilla.

2. Stir together baking powder, salt, and 3 cups flour; gradually add to butter mixture, beating just until blended. Spread three-fourths of batter in a greased and floured 13- x 9-inch baking pan; sprinkle with blackberries.

3. Stir together remaining ½ cup granulated sugar and ¼ cup flour in a medium bowl; add peaches and bourbon, stirring to coat. Spoon mixture over blackberries.

4. Stir pecans into remaining batter; dollop over peach mixture.

5. Bake at 350°F for 1 hour or until golden and bubbly. Cool completely on a wire rack (about 1 hour). Cut into bars.

SUNDAYS PAST & PRESENT
with ADRIAN MILLER

Meet Adrian Miller, attorney, politico, certified barbecue judge, and author of the James Beard Award-winning book *Soul Food: The Surprising Story of an American Cuisine, One Plate at a Time,* and *The President's Kitchen Cabinet.*

HOMETOWN: Denver, CO **RESIDES:** Denver, CO

WHAT COMES TO MIND WHEN YOU THINK OF MEALS FROM SUNDAYS PAST?

While I was growing up, we were pretty good about having dinner together as a family during the week and on the weekends. Sundays were no different. Sundays were special because my mother, who is a very good cook, would take dishes to the next level—especially the homemade desserts.

WHAT DISH DID YOU LOOK FORWARD TO HAVING?

Though soul food and Southern food were the main cuisines that I grew up eating, my mother was great at making other types of food. I remember looking forward to two dishes in particular. The first is a calzone—a classic Italian turnover. My mom's version used hot roll mix which she made into a dough, broke down into individual portions, rolled out into a flattened circle, and filled with hamburger, Italian sausage, and mozzarella cheese. The dough was then folded over to envelop the mixture to create a turnover that was baked. She served it with a marinara sauce that we poured over it. The other dish that I looked forward to was lemon icebox pie made with a crushed vanilla wafer crust, a lemony custard filling, and a baked meringue on top. That's the one all of the kids really wanted.

TELL US ABOUT YOUR FAVORITE SUNDAY SUPPER—PAST OR PRESENT.

My family saved the spectacular soul food spreads for Thanksgiving and New Year's Day. My favorite Sunday meal was a steak dinner: a grilled T-bone steak with steamed green beans, a roll, and a baked potato topped off with a dollop of sour cream.

Slow cooking a prime rib in a smoker yields fork-tender, juicy meat. Use long-lasting hickory chunks in your smoker, instead of hickory chips, to eliminate frequent door openings. This beautiful roast sings with the piquant but smooth balsamic-fig sauce. This robust side dish of wild rice and earthy fennel sautéed in bacon drippings is finished off with toasted walnuts (or pecans). Complete the menu with the most decadent chocolate pound cake you will ever make. Buttermilk is the key.

Allow plenty of time to get the smoker going, knowing there are 6 hours ahead to fully smoke the roast. Make the cake early in the day, or make even further ahead and freeze. Defrost at room temperature and glaze before serving. The rice can also be made ahead and reheated before serving.

Smoked PRIME RIB

Serves 8 to 10   *Hands-on 20 minutes*   *Total 7 hours, 50 minutes*

Hickory wood chunks
4 garlic cloves, minced
1 tablespoon salt
2 tablespoons coarsely ground black pepper
1 tablespoon dried rosemary
1 teaspoon dried thyme
1 (6-pound) beef rib roast
1 ½ cups dry red wine
1 ½ cups red wine vinegar
½ cup olive oil

NO SMOKER? Roast prime rib at 450°F for 45 minutes; reduce oven temperature to 350°F, and cook 45 minutes or until a meat thermometer inserted in thickest portion registers 145°F (medium-rare) or to desired degree of doneness. Remove from oven, cover loosely with aluminum foil, and let stand 15 minutes before slicing.

1. Soak wood chunks in water 1 hour.

2. Combine minced garlic and next 4 ingredients, and rub garlic mixture evenly over beef roast.

3. Stir together dry red wine, red wine vinegar, and olive oil; set wine mixture aside.

4. Prepare charcoal fire in smoker; let burn 15 to 20 minutes.

5. Drain wood chunks, and place on coals. Place water pan in smoker, and add water to just below fill line. Place beef roast in center on lower food rack. Gradually pour wine mixture over beef roast.

6. Cook beef roast, covered, 6 hours or until a meat thermometer inserted into thickest portion of beef roast registers 145°F (medium), adding more water to depth of fill line, if necessary. Remove beef roast from smoker, and let stand 15 minutes before slicing.

Wild Rice with
BACON AND FENNEL

Serves 8   *Hands-on 40 minutes*   *Total 1 hour, 5 minutes*

1 ⅓ cups uncooked wild rice
4 bacon slices
1 large fennel bulb, thinly sliced
1 large onion, cut into thin wedges
2 garlic cloves, minced
½ cup reduced-sodium fat-free chicken broth
⅓ cup golden raisins
¼ teaspoon salt
⅛ teaspoon freshly ground black pepper
¼ cup chopped fresh fennel fronds or flat-leaf parsley
1 tablespoon white wine vinegar
½ cup chopped toasted walnuts

1. Cook wild rice according to package directions; drain.

2. Meanwhile, cook bacon in a large nonstick skillet over medium-high heat 7 to 8 minutes or until crisp; drain on paper towels, reserving 1 tablespoon drippings in skillet. Chop bacon.

3. Sauté sliced fennel and onion in hot drippings over medium-high heat 5 minutes or until softened. Add garlic; sauté 1 minute. Add broth and next 3 ingredients; bring to a boil. Reduce heat to medium-low; cover and simmer 8 minutes or until tender. Stir in rice and bacon; cook, stirring often, 3 minutes.

4. Transfer to a large serving bowl. Stir in fennel fronds and vinegar. Stir in walnuts just before serving.

Peanut Butter and Jam
PIE BARS

Makes 24 bars   *Hands-on 15 minutes*
Total 1 hour, 10 minutes

½ cup creamy peanut butter
½ cup plus ⅓ cup butter, softened
½ cup granulated sugar
1½ cups firmly packed brown sugar
2 large eggs
1 teaspoon vanilla extract
1 teaspoon baking powder
2¼ cups all-purpose flour
¾ teaspoon salt
2 cups Strawberry-Lemonade Jam (page 90)
½ cup chopped dry-roasted peanuts

1. Preheat oven to 350°F. Beat peanut butter and ⅓ cup butter at medium speed with an electric mixer until creamy. Add granulated sugar and ½ cup brown sugar, beating well. Add eggs and vanilla; beat until blended. Combine baking powder, 1¼ cups flour, and ½ teaspoon salt; stir into peanut butter mixture just until blended. Press mixture onto bottom of a 15- x 10-inch jelly-roll pan. Bake at 350°F for 20 minutes or until edges are lightly browned. Cool 5 minutes; spread with jam.

2. Combine peanuts, remaining 1 cup brown sugar, 1 cup flour, ½ cup butter, and ¼ teaspoon salt in a small bowl with a pastry blender until crumbly. Sprinkle topping over jam. Bake at 350°F for 30 minutes or until topping is lightly browned. Serve warm or at room temperature.

Homemade jam or preserves make a delicious filling for these decadent pie bars. Feel free to use the remaining Strawberry-Lemonade Jam here, adding additional strawberry jam to make the 2 cups needed for the bars. And store-bought jams are just fine, too.

MENU FIVE

SERVES 8

We have a natural affinity for foods cooked on an open fire, and all the better if they are on a stick. Thread your skewers with chicken or steak, or prepare some of both. The dry rub is a sweet-and-spicy mixture with a base of brown sugar, kicked up with chipotle chile powder. A true Alabama original, white barbecue sauce has spread its appeal beyond the state and is seen served with barbecued chicken all around the South. This is a mild version, complementing the kabobs perfectly. Jalapeño peppers and lime juice and zest combine to punch up the butter served on the corn. Ice-cream floats win over everyone in the crowd. The chicken can be threaded and sprinkled with the rub early in the day and kept refrigerated until grilling. Prepare the white barbecue sauce and jalapeño-lime butter early as well. Grill the corn first, as it can sit a few minutes while the kabobs are cooking. The floats can be self-serve: Everyone loves to make their own.

BARBECUE KABOBS (page 95)

GRILLED JALAPEÑO-LIME
CORN ON THE COB (page 96)

FIZZY FRUITY
ICE-CREAM FLOATS (page 98)

SET THE
SCENE

Make it a Fourth of July Shindig!

Hardly a soul can resist a cookout on the big summer holiday celebrating our nation's independence. American flags and patriotic bunting adorn porches and decks, while guests are decked out in the colors of the day.

Break out your reds, whites, and blues for colorful table adornments as well, and mix and match the shades while you're at it. String lights on this festive day for a party atmosphere as the sun goes down. Set the table with small bottles containing Queen Anne's lace, bountiful at this time of year. Light a sparkler in each one as the fireworks show begins.

Nothing beats a small-town parade, and if you've never attended one, put it on your bucket list. Homemade floats, ribbon-festooned bicycles, antique cars, and big shiny fire trucks all roll single file down main street, thrilling those young and old.

Every grill in town will be fired up for the celebration. If you are planning for a crowd, these recipes can easily multiply to match your guest list.

With all the colorful festivities going on and this bounty of prepared food, be sure to take lots of pictures. You can have a family photo contest with your own unique hashtag. The photo with the most likes wins the day!

BARBECUE KABOBS

Serves 8   Hands-on 20 minutes   Total 38 minutes, including rub and sauce

2 pounds skinned and boned chicken breasts,
  or 2 pounds top sirloin steak, trimmed
½ large red onion, cut into fourths and
  separated into pieces
1 pint cherry tomatoes
8 (8-inch) metal skewers
Smoky Barbecue Rub
White Barbecue Sauce

1. Preheat grill to 350° to 400°F (medium-high) heat. Cut chicken into 1-inch cubes. Thread chicken, onion, and tomatoes alternately onto skewers, leaving a ¼-inch space between pieces. Sprinkle kabobs with Smoky Barbecue Rub.

2. Grill kabobs, covered with grill lid, 4 to 5 minutes on each side. Serve with White Barbecue Sauce.

Smoky Barbecue Rub

Makes ¼ cup   Hands-on 5 minutes   Total 5 minutes

2 tablespoons firmly packed dark brown sugar
2 teaspoons garlic salt
1 teaspoon chipotle chile powder
½ teaspoon ground cumin
¼ teaspoon dried oregano

Stir together brown sugar, garlic salt, chipotle chile powder, cumin, and oregano.

White Barbecue Sauce

Makes 1 ¾ cups   Hands-on 5 minutes   Total 5 minutes

½ cup mayonnaise
⅓ cup white vinegar
1 teaspoon freshly ground black pepper
½ teaspoon salt
½ teaspoon sugar
1 garlic clove, pressed

Stir together mayonnaise, vinegar, pepper, salt, sugar, and garlic. Refrigerate until needed.

Grilled Jalapeño–Lime
CORN ON THE COB

Serves 8   *Hands-on 15 minutes*   *Total 30 minutes*

8 ears fresh corn, husks removed
Vegetable cooking spray
½ cup butter, softened
1 jalapeño pepper, seeded and minced
1 small garlic clove, pressed
1 tablespoon lime zest
1 tablespoon fresh lime juice
2 teaspoons chopped fresh cilantro

1. Preheat grill to 350° to 400°F (medium-high) heat. Coat corn lightly with cooking spray. Sprinkle with salt and pepper to taste. Grill corn, covered with grill lid, 15 minutes or until golden brown, turning occasionally.

2. Meanwhile, stir together butter and next 5 ingredients. Remove corn from grill, and cut into thirds. Serve corn with butter mixture.

Make shucking even easier by cooking the corn just 1½ minutes on HIGH in a microwave. The silks will just peel away like magic.

SUNDAYS PAST & PRESENT
with MAGGIE GREEN

Meet Maggie Green, food writer and author of *The Kentucky Fresh Cookbook.*
HOMETOWN: Lexington, KY **RESIDES:** Northern Kentucky

WHAT COMES TO MIND WHEN YOU THINK OF MEALS FROM SUNDAYS PAST?

Sundays past were "Walt-Disney-and-split-a-Coke" kind of days that revolved around my family's weekly Sunday routine. Every week on Sunday morning we attended Mass at our local parish church. When we returned home, Mom read the paper while Dad watched *Meet the Press* or *Star Trek.* I either joined my dad in the TV room or did some homework I'd put off since Friday afternoon. Often Dad offered to take us on a Sunday drive. Dad was a civil engineer, and he designed bridges for Kentucky's interstate system. So, if we didn't end up at the site of a half-finished bridge, we'd visit my aunt's farm two counties away. Once home, Mom then turned to the kitchen while my sisters and I set the table for 10. After supper we were expected to clean up the kitchen. Once everything quieted down, we settled in the TV room, hoping to pick the biggest floor pillow, because at 7 p.m. the *Wonderful World of Disney* and a glass of Coca-Cola were served. I have fond memories of Sunday: my soda for the week and a day with my mom, dad, and siblings.

WHAT DISH DID YOU LOOK FORWARD TO HAVING?

Mom leaned on German-inspired foods, along with ground beef, to keep my father's food idiosyncrasies in check. Pork roast, weiner schnitzel, bread dumplings, meatloaf, spaghetti, red cabbage, mashed potatoes, and coleslaw were common for Sunday suppers. My favorite was pork roast and the bread dumplings my German grandfather taught Mom how to make. They were made from bread, and the dough was shaped in a cylinder, then rolled and tied in a white linen napkin. The whole dumpling, napkin and all, was boiled in broth, then sliced to serve with the pork roast and homemade brown gravy.

TELL US ABOUT YOUR FAVORITE SUNDAY SUPPER—PAST OR PRESENT.

My favorite Sunday suppers now are when all my children are home and we eat together, weather permitting, on our patio as the sun sets behind our house. On the menu is one of my favorite summer Sunday suppers: grilled chicken thighs with lemon-garlic olive oil; a grill wok combination of fresh squash, onions, and mushrooms; corn on the cob; sliced tomato and mozzarella salad; and grilled bread. The feeling is the same: home, family, together. I'm pleased that we still enjoy "Walt-Disney-and-split-a-Coke" Sundays in our home, with our own children. To me, that's what Sundays are all about.

Grilling on cedar planks imparts a woodsy, slightly smoky flavor to these salmon fillets. Cedar planks are found in grocery stores and cookware shops. Avoid the lumberyard unless the wood is certified non-treated with chemicals. Roasted carrots have a natural sweetness, and the little bit of sorghum or honey aids the caramelization of the carrots without becoming overly sweet. Avocados, cilantro, and pepitas (pumpkin seeds) top off this colorful side dish. Individual tarts make impressive desserts. The vanilla-buttermilk custard uses vanilla bean paste, found in many grocery stores and specialty shops. The paste is made from the scrapings from inside the pod and will send tiny flecks of vanilla seeds throughout the custard. Top the tarts with fresh fruit and basil sprigs for an eye-catching garnish. Soak the planks and make the custard filling early in the day. The baked tart shells and the roasted carrots can sit at room temperature a couple of hours ahead. Assemble the carrot dish just before the fish is ready to come off the grill. Fill the tarts just before serving to prevent the shells from becoming soggy.

Lemon Grilled
SALMON

Serves 4   *Hands-on 15 minutes*   *Total 8 hours, 30 minutes*

2 (15- x 6-inch) cedar grilling planks
3 tablespoons chopped fresh dill
3 tablespoons chopped fresh parsley
2 teaspoons grated lemon rind
3 tablespoons fresh lemon juice
1 tablespoon olive oil
1 garlic clove, pressed
½ teaspoon salt
¼ teaspoon freshly ground black pepper
4 (6-ounce) salmon fillets

1. Weigh down cedar planks with a heavier object in a large container. Add water to cover, and soak at least 8 hours.

2. Combine dill and next 5 ingredients; set aside. Sprinkle salt and pepper evenly on salmon.

3. Remove cedar planks from water, and place planks on cooking grate on grill.

4. Grill soaked planks, covered with grill lid, over medium-high (350° to 400°F) heat 2 minutes or until the planks begin to lightly smoke. Place 2 fillets skin side down on each cedar plank, and grill, covered with grill lid, 15 to 18 minutes or until fish flakes with a fork. Carefully remove planks from grill using tongs, and remove fish from planks to individual serving plates using a spatula. Spoon herb mixture over fish, and serve immediately.

Roasted Carrots with Avocado and Feta
VINAIGRETTE

Serves 4   *Hands-on 20 minutes*   *Total 35 minutes*

2 pounds small carrots in assorted colors
1 tablespoon sorghum syrup or honey
4 tablespoons extra virgin olive oil
1 teaspoon kosher salt
1 teaspoon ground cumin
½ teaspoon freshly ground black pepper
¼ teaspoon dried crushed red pepper
1 shallot, minced
2 tablespoons red wine vinegar
2 ounces feta, blue, or goat cheese, crumbled
1 medium-size ripe avocado, sliced
2 tablespoons fresh cilantro leaves
1 tablespoon roasted, salted, and shelled pepitas (pumpkin seeds)

1. Preheat oven to 500°F. Toss carrots with sorghum and 2 tablespoons olive oil. Sprinkle with kosher salt and next 3 ingredients; toss to coat. Place carrots in a lightly greased jelly-roll pan.

2. Bake at 500°F for 15 to 20 minutes or until tender, stirring halfway through.

3. Stir together shallot and vinegar. Add salt and pepper to taste. Stir in remaining 2 tablespoons olive oil; stir in feta.

4. Arrange carrots and avocado on a serving platter. Drizzle with vinaigrette. Sprinkle with cilantro and pepitas.

The key to roasting veggies is to use similarly sized pieces. Spread them evenly on a baking sheet, and roast in a very hot oven until just tender.

Vanilla–Buttermilk TARTS

Makes 8 tarts   *Hands-on 30 minutes*   *Total 5 hours*

⅔ cup sugar
¼ cup all-purpose flour
1½ cups buttermilk
3 large eggs
2 teaspoons vanilla bean paste
1 (8- or 10-ounce) package frozen tart shells
Toppings: fresh fruit, fresh basil sprigs

1. Whisk together sugar and flour in a 3-quart heavy saucepan; add buttermilk and eggs, and whisk until blended. Cook over medium heat, whisking constantly, 7 to 8 minutes or until a pudding-like thickness. Remove from heat, and stir in vanilla bean paste. Cover and chill 4 to 24 hours.

2. Meanwhile, bake frozen tart shells according to package directions, and cool completely (about 30 minutes). Spoon custard into tart shells, and top with desired toppings just before serving.

MENU SEVEN

SERVES 4

SHRIMP AND VEGETABLE RICE (PAGE 105)

SESAME WONTON CRISPS (PAGE 106)

EASY BERRY COBBLER (PAGE 107)

Grilled vegetables in fragrant jasmine rice are served as a bed under grilled marinated shrimp. The shrimp is marinated in red pepper jelly, hot chili sauce, and lime juice for a sweet-spicy flavor. Jasmine rice is cooked in garlic and coconut milk and studded with grilled corn, chopped roasted peppers, and grilled onion. Prepare the wonton crisps early in the day, cool, and store in an airtight container. Start the grill an hour or so before you want to serve. Put the cobbler in the oven just before dining, or while grilling, and set aside to cool.

Shrimp and Vegetable
RICE

Serves 4 to 6   *Hands-on 25 minutes*   *Total 1 hour, 5 minutes*

1 (13.66-ounce) can coconut milk
2 garlic cloves, minced
1 teaspoon salt
3 tablespoons red pepper jelly
2 tablespoons olive oil
1 teaspoon Asian hot chili sauce (such as Sriracha)
1 teaspoon lime zest
6 tablespoons fresh lime juice
2 pounds peeled, large raw shrimp
1¼ cups uncooked jasmine rice
2 ears fresh corn
5 assorted mini bell peppers
1 sweet onion, cut into ½-inch slices
2 teaspoons olive oil
½ cup chopped fresh herbs (such as flat-leaf parsley, mint, basil, and cilantro)

1. Preheat grill to 350° to 400°F (medium-high) heat. Bring first 3 ingredients and ⅔ cup water to a boil in a medium saucepan over high heat.

2. While coconut milk mixture comes to a boil, whisk together red pepper jelly, next 3 ingredients, and ¼ cup fresh lime juice in a bowl. Reserve 2 tablespoons jelly mixture. Combine remaining jelly mixture and shrimp. Let stand 20 minutes.

3. Meanwhile, stir rice into boiling coconut milk mixture. Cover, reduce heat to low, and simmer 20 minutes or until liquid is absorbed. Remove from heat, and keep covered.

4. While shrimp marinates and rice simmers, brush corn, peppers, and onion with 2 teaspoons olive oil, and grill, covered with grill lid, 8 minutes or until slightly charred, turning halfway through. Remove and discard seeds from peppers; chop peppers. Cut kernels from corn cobs. Discard cobs. Chop onion. Combine peppers, corn, and onion in a bowl.

5. Remove shrimp from marinade, discarding marinade. Grill shrimp, covered with grill lid, 3 minutes on each side or just until shrimp turn pink. Remove shrimp from grill; sprinkle with 1 tablespoon lime juice, and toss with reserved 2 tablespoons jelly mixture. Stir remaining 1 tablespoon lime juice into rice. Stir rice mixture and herbs into grilled vegetables. Serve remaining shrimp over rice-and-vegetable mixture.

Sesame WONTON CRISPS

Makes 12 pieces   *Hands-on 5 minutes*   *Total 10 minutes*

12 wonton wrappers
1 tablespoon melted butter
½ teaspoon white sesame seeds
½ teaspoon black sesame seeds
¼ teaspoon kosher salt

1. Preheat oven to 425°F. Place wonton wrappers on an ungreased baking sheet. Brush 1 side of each wrapper with melted butter; sprinkle with sesame seeds and salt.

2. Bake at 425°F for 5 to 6 minutes or until golden brown.

Note: Wonton wrappers can be found in the refrigerated produce section of most supermarkets.

Easy Berry
COBBLER

Serves 6   Hands-on 10 minutes   Total 1 hour

4 cups frozen blackberries
1 tablespoon lemon juice
1 large egg
1 cup sugar
1 cup all-purpose flour
6 tablespoons butter, melted
Sweetened whipped cream (optional)

1. Preheat oven to 375°F. Place blackberries in a lightly greased 8-inch squaand flour in a medium bowl until mixture resembles coarse meal. Sprinkle over fruit. Drizzle melted butter over topping.

2. Bake at 375°F for 40 to 45 minutes or until lightly browned and bubbly. Let stand 10 minutes. Serve warm with sweetened whipped cream, if desired.

For individual cobblers, prepare recipe as directed and divide between 6 (8-ounce) ramekins. Bake exactly as directed (same temperature and same time) on an aluminum foil-lined baking sheet.

Variation

EASY PEACH COBBLER
Substitute 4 cups frozen sliced peaches for blackberries. Prepare recipe as directed, sprinkling 1 tablespoon peach schnapps and ½ teaspoon ground cinnamon over peaches with lemon juice, and baking cobbler 1 hour to 1 hour and 5 minutes or until lightly browned and bubbly.

MENU EIGHT
SERVES 8

SHRIMP TACOS (PAGE 109)

WATERMELON AND FENNEL SALAD WITH HONEY-LIME VINAIGRETTE (PAGE 110)

ICEBOX BUTTER COOKIES (PAGE 111)

For this menu, large shrimp are tossed in a bit of ancho chili powder and cumin, and then grilled to perfection. Nestled on a bed of shredded cabbage and grated carrots, and tucked into a warm taco, this meal can be dressed up with a little hot sauce, Mexican crema or regular sour cream, and chopped radishes. Cool and crisp, this salad is perfect on a hot day. Tangy feta and the clean flavors of mint and lime balance the sweet watermelon. The crunchy fennel has a slight anise flavor. A delicious alternative to traditional lemon versions, the vinaigrette would also enhance grilled fish or chicken. And the butter cookies reign supreme in the icebox cookie category. Rich and, of course, buttery, these cookies are outstanding, but also try the lemon-basil variation for a modern take on a classic.

Prepare the butter cookie dough up to three days in advance or at least eight hours before baking. The salad can be made early in the day, but reserve the mint and cheese for topping the salad just before serving. The tacos are best hot off the grill.

SHRIMP TACOS

Serves 8   Hands-on 15 minutes   Total 35 minutes

10 to 12 (10-inch) wooden skewers
2 pounds unpeeled, large raw shrimp
Vegetable cooking spray
2 tablespoons hot sauce
1 tablespoon olive oil
1 ½ teaspoons ancho chile powder
1 ½ teaspoons ground cumin
¾ teaspoon salt
16 to 20 (8-inch) soft taco-size corn or flour tortillas
3 cups shredded cabbage
1 cup grated carrots
Lime wedges

1. Soak skewers in water 20 minutes.

2. Meanwhile, peel shrimp; devein, if desired. Coat cold cooking grate of grill with cooking spray, and place on grill. Preheat grill to 350° to 400°F (medium-high) heat.

3. Toss shrimp with hot sauce and next 4 ingredients. Thread shrimp onto skewers. Grill shrimp, covered with grill lid, 1 to 2 minutes on each side or just until shrimp turn pink. Grill tortillas 1 minute on each side or until warmed.

4. Combine cabbage and carrots. Remove shrimp from skewers just before serving. Serve shrimp in warm tortillas with cabbage mixture and lime wedges.

Watermelon and
FENNEL SALAD
with Honey – Lime Vinaigrette

Serves 8   *Hands-on 10 minutes*   *Total 10 minutes*

3 tablespoons fresh lime juice
2 tablespoons olive oil
1 tablespoon honey
¼ teaspoon kosher salt
¼ teaspoon freshly ground black pepper
1 tablespoon finely minced shallots
3 ¼ cups thinly sliced fennel bulb
3 cups cubed watermelon
¼ cup chopped fresh mint
2 ounces crumbled feta cheese (about ½ cup)

Combine first 5 ingredients, stirring with a whisk. Stir in shallots. Combine fennel and watermelon in a large bowl. Drizzle dressing over watermelon mixture; toss gently. Sprinkle with mint and cheese.

Icebox Butter
COOKIES

Makes 8 to 10 dozen **Hands-on 20 minutes**
Total 8 hours, 48 minutes

1 cup butter, softened
1½ cups granulated sugar
½ cup firmly packed light brown sugar
1 tablespoon vanilla extract
2 large eggs
3½ cups all-purpose flour
½ teaspoon baking soda
½ teaspoon salt
Parchment paper

1. Beat first 4 ingredients at medium speed with an electric mixer until fluffy. Add eggs, 1 at a time, beating just until blended after each addition.

2. Stir together flour and next 2 ingredients; gradually add to butter mixture, beating just until blended after each addition.

3. Shape dough into 4 logs (about 2 inches in diameter); wrap each log in plastic wrap. Chill 8 hours or up to 3 days.

4. Preheat oven to 350°F. Cut each log into ¼-inch-thick slices; place on parchment paper–lined baking sheets. Bake 8 to 12 minutes or until lightly browned. Remove from baking sheets to wire racks, and cool completely (about 20 minutes).

Variation

LEMON-BASIL
Add ¼ cup finely chopped fresh basil, 2 tablespoons lemon zest, and 2 tablespoons poppy seeds with first 4 ingredients.

Bake 8 minutes for a soft and chewy cookie or up to 12 minutes for a crisp cookie.

MENU NINE

SERVES 4-6

GRILLED SAUSAGES WITH ASPARAGUS (PAGE 113)

STRAWBERRY-TOMATO SALAD (PAGE 114)

STRAWBERRY SHORTCAKE (PAGE 115)

Here is just the right menu when you want strawberry season to last forever. The sausages and asparagus may be the main course, but the salad and shortcake could steal the show. Select your favorite sausage for this dish, be it chorizo, sweet or spicy Italian, or the turkey and chicken varieties available at the grocery store, and consult the package regarding the correct temperatures for doneness. The salad highlights summer at its very best and needs nothing but a sprinkling of fresh herbs and lemon zest. Served as a two-layer cake, the strawberry shortcake is a thing of beauty. Coating the layers with beaten egg white, then sprinkling with sugar gives each layer a browned and glistening surface.

The shortcake layers can be baked earlier in the day. Plan ahead for slicing and chilling the strawberries. Assemble cake with whipped cream just before serving. Prepare the salad and leave it at room temperature before preheating the grill. The sausages and asparagus are best served hot off the grill.

GRILLED SAUSAGES
with Asparagus

Serves 4 to 6   *Hands-on 20 minutes*   *Total 35 minutes*

3 lemons, halved
½ cup refrigerated pesto sauce
½ cup toasted walnuts, chopped
2 pounds fresh asparagus
2 tablespoons olive oil
2 pounds sweet Italian sausage links

1. Preheat grill to medium-high (350° to 400°F) heat. Squeeze juice from 2 lemon halves to equal 2 tablespoons. Stir together pesto, lemon juice, and ¼ cup walnuts. Snap off and discard tough ends of asparagus; toss asparagus with olive oil.

2. Grill sausage, without grill lid, 10 minutes or until thoroughly cooked, turning occasionally. At the same time, grill asparagus, without grill lid, 4 minutes or until tender. Brush asparagus with pesto mixture and transfer to a serving platter. Grill remaining 4 lemon halves, cut sides down, 1 minute or until charred. Place on platter with asparagus. Slice sausage, and arrange on serving platter. Sprinkle with remaining ¼ cup walnuts.

Strawberry – Tomato
SALAD

Serves 6   *Hands-on 15 minutes*   *Total 15 minutes*

1 ½ cups fresh strawberries, chopped
½ pound assorted small heirloom tomatoes, quartered
⅓ cup chopped fresh basil
1 tablespoon chopped fresh oregano
1 teaspoon loosely packed lemon zest
½ teaspoon kosher salt
¼ teaspoon freshly ground black pepper

Stir together all ingredients. Serve at room temperature.

Select fresh heirloom tomatoes by sight, smell, and heft. Look for smooth skins, a pleasant fragrance, and ones that are heavy for their size. And never refrigerate them.

The results of these Cajun – seasoned baby back pork ribs smoked on the grill are worth the effort. Heavenly to behold and a pleasure to eat, the sweet corn pudding is a Southern casserole at its best. Fresh corn is ideal, but frozen corn (3 to 4 cups) will work in this recipe as well. Begin smoking the ribs about 6 hours before supper time, and prepare the casserole to come out of the oven when the ribs are due to be ready. Blend the base for this cold and sparkly spritzer ahead, pour into a pitcher, and refrigerate until needed. Add club soda just before serving.

Smoky
RIBS

Serrves 6   *Hands-on 30 minutes*   *Total 6 hours, 15 minutes*

3 slabs baby back pork ribs (about 6 pounds)
Hickory wood chunks
¼ cup Cajun seasoning
Bottled barbecue sauce

1. Rinse and pat ribs dry. Remove thin membrane from back of ribs by slicing into it with a knife and then pulling. (This makes for more tender ribs and allows smoke and rub to penetrate meat better.) Soak wood chunks in water for 1 hour.

2. Sprinkle meat evenly with Cajun seasoning, and massage into meat. Let stand at room temperature 30 minutes.

3. Prepare smoker according to manufacturer's directions. Bring internal temperature to 225° to 250°F; maintain temperature for 15 to 20 minutes.

4. Drain wood chunks, and place on coals. Place rib slabs in a rib rack on upper cooking grate; cover with smoker lid.

5. Smoke ribs, maintaining temperature in smoker between 225° and 250°F, for 3½ to 4 hours. Remove ribs from grill, and wrap in heavy-duty aluminum foil; return ribs to smoker. Cover with smoker lid, and smoke 30 more minutes. Serve with barbecue sauce.

Soak wood chips in water at least 30 minutes and wood chunks 1 to 24 hours before grilling. Start your fire, and let coals burn down until they're covered with gray ash. Cover coals with soaked chips, and set smoker vents to produce a smooth, even draft.

Sweet Corn
PUDDING

Serves 6 to 8   Hands-on 30 minutes
Total 1 hour, 15 minutes

9 ears fresh corn, husks removed
4 large eggs, lightly beaten
½ cup half-and-half
1½ teaspoons baking powder
⅓ cup butter
2 tablespoons sugar
2 tablespoons all-purpose flour
1 tablespoon butter, melted
⅛ teaspoon freshly ground black pepper

1. Preheat oven to 350°F. Cut off tips of corn kernels into a bowl; scrape milk and remaining pulp from cob with a paring knife to measure 3 to 4 cups.

2. Whisk together eggs, half-and-half, and baking powder until well combined.

3. Melt ⅓ cup butter in a large saucepan over low heat; add sugar and flour, whisking until smooth. Remove from heat; gradually add egg mixture, whisking constantly until smooth. Stir in corn. Pour corn mixture into a greased 1- or 1½-quart baking dish.

4. Bake at 350°F for 40 to 45 minutes or until pudding is set. Drizzle with 1 tablespoon butter; sprinkle with pepper.

5. Increase heat to broil. Broil pudding 5½ inches from heat 2 minutes or until golden. Let stand 5 minutes before serving.

Strawberry Margarita SPRITZERS

Makes about 8 cups   *Hands-on 10 minutes*
Total 10 minutes

1 (10-ounce) package frozen whole strawberries, thawed
1 (10-ounce) can frozen strawberry daiquiri mix, thawed
1 cup tequila
¼ cup orange liqueur
2 tablespoons fresh lime juice
1 (1-liter) bottle club soda, chilled

Pulse first 5 ingredients in a blender until smooth. Pour into a pitcher, and stir in club soda just before serving. Serve over ice.

For a party, make a few batches without adding the club soda. Place in zip-top plastic freezer bags and freeze. Remove from the freezer, and let stand a few minutes before adding the club soda.

Chapter 3

COMPANY'S CALLING

Picnics, backyard or poolside, kitchen table or dining room — it doesn't really matter where, we just want to be together. I marveled at the ease with which my friend pulled together an impromptu supper recently. I had dropped by for a visit in the afternoon and shortly after, two more friends came. Then calls went out to the husbands to bring wine. A spontaneous dinner party was born. We stayed in the kitchen as my friend chopped and cooked and stirred risotto. She was excellent at allowing extra hands in the kitchen, and suddenly a big salad was made and a cobbler was in the oven. I am the queen of organization and love to have my menu planned in advance, and I keep a well-stocked pantry. But my friend has inspired me to be more spontaneous. With candles lit and cloth napkins at our places, it appeared as though this had been a well-thought-out plan all along.

These recipes are for both the planners and the spontaneous. The large cuts of meat clearly require advanced planning—*Herb-Roasted Boneless Leg of Lamb* and *Herb-and-Potato-Chip-Crusted Beef Tenderloin*. And others can be made ahead—*5-Ingredient Slow-Cooker Pulled Pork, Hearty Italian Soup,* or *Baked Ziti with Sausage.* And then there are the long-cooking recipes made just for Sunday cooking—*Chicken-and-Brisket Brunswick Stew, Louisiana Gumbo, Rosemary-Garlic Chicken Quarters,* and so much more.

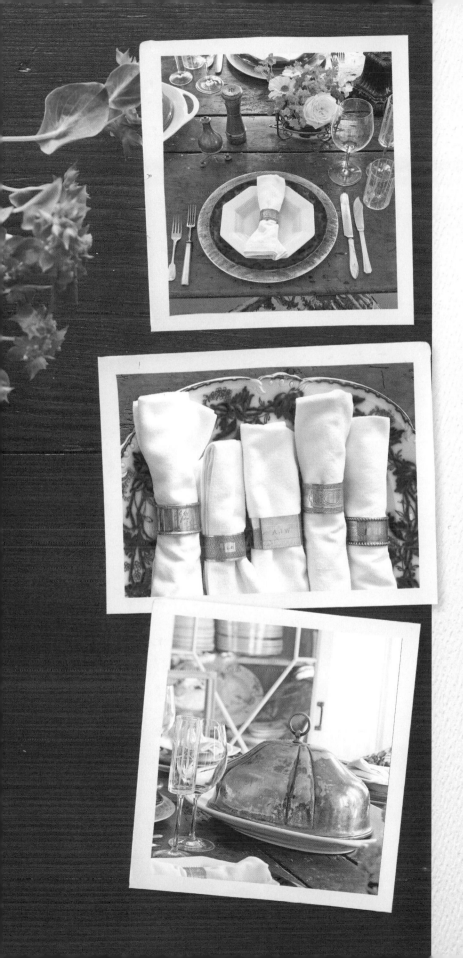

SET THE
SCENE

Truly formal dining is rarely seen these days, as most of us do not have hired waitstaff or kitchen assistants to provide general service functions and to set and clear courses.

But having been left to our own devices, we have managed well. Setting the table is part of the fun of planning an event. For a seated supper, break out the silver—mismatched is chic—and use favorite serving pieces. Keep the tablescape low so as not to block the conversation across the table. The same goes for the candlesticks—they should be either high or low. No matter how mix-and-match I go, I always bring my table together with matching napkins. Generously large white linen dinner napkins are easily found in vintage shops and secondhand stores and are my napkin of choice for a seated meal. Napkin rings add a special touch.

Tablescapes add so much personality to the table and don't have to be a stressor for the host. A decorative platter, bowl, or low basket of colorful and seasonal fresh fruits and vegetables is always a winner. A clear glass bowl of lemons, limes, or oranges creates a clean, minimalist look for the table—just match the citrus to the menu. For my narrow dining table, small flowering branches down the center of the table interspersed with votive candles are a simple but elegant choice.

Herb-and-Potato-Chip-Crusted
BEEF TENDERLOIN

Serves 6 to 8   Hands-on 40 minutes   Total 2 hours, 40 minutes, including chutney

1 (4- to 5-pound) beef tenderloin, trimmed
3 teaspoons kosher salt
¾ cup panko (Japanese breadcrumbs)
3 garlic cloves, pressed
2 teaspoons coarsely ground black pepper
3 tablespoons olive oil
1¼ cups crushed, plain kettle-cooked potato chips
¼ cup finely chopped fresh parsley
1 tablespoon finely chopped fresh thyme
1 bay leaf, crushed
1 egg white, lightly beaten
1 tablespoon Dijon mustard
Cherry Chutney

1. Preheat oven to 400°F. Sprinkle tenderloin with 2 teaspoons salt. Let stand 30 to 45 minutes.

2. Meanwhile, sauté panko, garlic, 1 teaspoon pepper, and remaining 1 teaspoon salt in 1 tablespoon hot oil in a skillet over medium heat 2 to 3 minutes or until deep golden brown. Let cool completely (about 10 minutes). Stir in potato chips and next 4 ingredients.

3. Pat tenderloin dry with paper towels, and sprinkle with remaining 1 teaspoon pepper. Brown beef in remaining 2 tablespoons hot oil in a roasting pan over medium-high heat until browned on all sides (about 2 to 3 minutes per side). Transfer tenderloin to a wire rack in an aluminum foil-lined jelly-roll pan. Let stand 10 minutes.

4. Spread mustard over tenderloin. Press panko mixture onto top and sides.

5. Bake at 400°F for 40 to 45 minutes or until coating is crisp and a meat thermometer inserted into thickest portion registers 130°F (rare). Let stand 10 minutes. Serve with Cherry Chutney.

Cherry Chutney

Makes about ½ cup   Hands-on 20 minutes   Total 20 minutes

2 tablespoons butter
1½ cups diced red bell pepper
¼ cup thinly sliced green onions
½ cup coarsely chopped dried cherries
3 tablespoons balsamic vinegar
2 teaspoons brown sugar
1 teaspoon finely chopped thyme

Melt butter in a large skillet over medium heat. Stir in bell pepper and green onions; cook, stirring occasionally, 12 to 15 minutes or until browned and tender. Stir in cherries, balsamic vinegar, brown sugar, and thyme. Cook, stirring often, 2 to 5 minutes or until slightly thickened. Add salt and pepper to taste.

Sweet Potato, Cauliflower, and
GREENS CASSEROLE

Serves 6 to 8   *Hands-on 55 minutes*   *Total 1 hour, 55 minutes, including cheese sauce*

1 head cauliflower (1½ to 2 pounds), cut into small florets

1 (8-ounce) package fresh cremini mushrooms, stemmed and halved

6 tablespoons olive oil

1 teaspoon ground cumin

1 teaspoon kosher salt

¼ teaspoon freshly ground black pepper

3 large sweet potatoes (2½ to 3 pounds), peeled and cut into ¼-inch-thick slices

2 garlic cloves, minced

4 cups chopped fresh kale, collards, or mustard greens

2 teaspoons red wine vinegar

1 (14-ounce) can butter beans, drained and rinsed (optional)

Easy Cheese Sauce

½ cup panko (Japanese breadcrumbs)

1 tablespoon chopped cilantro

1 teaspoon extra virgin olive oil

1. Preheat oven to 475°F. Toss together cauliflower, mushrooms, 2½ tablespoons oil, ½ teaspoon cumin, ½ teaspoon salt, and ⅛ teaspoon pepper in a medium bowl. Spread cauliflower mixture in a single layer in jelly-roll pan.

2. Toss together sweet potatoes, 2½ tablespoons oil, and remaining cumin, salt, and pepper. Spread in a single layer in another jelly-roll pan. Bake potatoes and cauliflower at 475°F for 10 to 12 minutes or until browned and just tender, turning once. Cool on wire racks 10 minutes.

3. Reduce oven temperature to 375°F. Heat remaining 1 tablespoon oil in a large skillet over medium-high heat. Add garlic; cook, stirring often, 1 minute. Add kale; cook, stirring occasionally, 10 minutes or until tender. Add salt and pepper to taste; stir in vinegar.

4. Layer half each of sweet potatoes, cauliflower mixture, beans (if desired), kale, and 1½ cups Easy Cheese Sauce in a lightly greased 13- x 9-inch baking dish. Repeat layers once. Top with remaining ½ cup cheese sauce. Stir together panko, chopped cilantro, and olive oil, and sprinkle crumb mixture over casserole.

5. Bake at 375°F for 20 to 25 minutes or until thoroughly heated, bubbly, and golden brown. Let stand 5 minutes before serving.

Easy Cheese Sauce

Bring ⅓ cup vermouth (or dry sherry) and 1 garlic clove, minced, to a boil in a large skillet over medium-high heat; reduce heat to medium-low, and simmer 7 to 10 minutes or until vermouth is reduced to 1 tablespoon. Whisk together 3 cups half-and-half and 3 tablespoons cornstarch and whisk into vermouth mixture. Whisk in 1 teaspoon salt and ½ teaspoon freshly ground black pepper. Boil, whisking constantly, 1 minute or until mixture is thickened. Stir in 2 cups shredded pepper Jack cheese. Reduce heat to low. Simmer, whisking constantly, 1 minute or until sauce is smooth. Remove from heat, and use immediately.

Chocolate – Pecan
CHESS PIE

Serves 8　　　*Hands-on 15 minutes*　　　*Total 2 hours, 5 minutes*

½ (14.1-ounce) package refrigerated piecrusts
½ cup butter
2 (1-ounce) unsweetened chocolate baking squares
1 (5-ounce) can evaporated milk
2 large eggs
2 teaspoons vanilla extract
1½ cups granulated sugar

3 tablespoons unsweetened cocoa
2 tablespoons all-purpose flour
⅛ teaspoon salt
1½ cups pecan halves and pieces
⅔ cup firmly packed light brown sugar
1 tablespoon light corn syrup

1. Preheat oven to 350°F. Roll piecrust into a 13-inch circle on a lightly floured surface. Fit into a 9-inch pie plate; fold edges under, and crimp.

2. Microwave butter and chocolate squares in a large microwave-safe bowl at MEDIUM (50% power) 1½ minutes or until melted and smooth, stirring at 30-second intervals. Whisk in evaporated milk, eggs, and 1 teaspoon vanilla.

3. Stir together granulated sugar and next 3 ingredients. Add sugar mixture to chocolate mixture; whisking until smooth. Pour mixture into prepared crust. Bake pie at 350°F for 40 minutes. Stir together pecans, next 2 ingredients, and remaining 1 teaspoon vanilla; sprinkle over pie. Bake 10 more minutes or until set. Remove from oven to a wire rack, and cool completely (about 1 hour).

Shelled pecans will keep at least 6 months in the refrigerator or up to one year in the freezer. Because they absorb odors and flavors, store pecans in a sealed plastic bag or airtight container.

SOUTHERN SAVVY
FOOD ALLERGIES

Americans have embraced special diets like never before. Some of these are passing fads, but some are medically necessary due to severe allergies or other serious conditions. It's long been held as rude behavior for an invited guest to quiz the host about the proposed menu, but that rule has finally relaxed, and communication is key. As a host, ask your guests if they have a serious allergy you should know about. For guests, if you aren't asked by your host about allergies, a polite solution is to tell the host upon being invited that you'd love to attend but have a serious allergy, and ask if you could bring a dish to share.

SUNDAYS PAST & PRESENT
with DAMON LEE FOWLER

Meet Damon Lee Fowler, culinary historian, cookbook author, and nationally recognized authority on Southern cooking and its history.

HOMETOWN: Born in Newnan, GA; grew up in Gaffney and Clover, SC **RESIDES:** Savannah, GA

WHAT COMES TO MIND WHEN YOU THINK OF MEALS FROM SUNDAYS PAST?

My mother's Sunday dinner pot roast and banana pudding. Mama made great fried chicken, but we didn't have that all that often on Sunday. She usually baked it instead of frying it. But the thing we all loved and looked forward to was that pot roast. She loved it because she could put it together before church and leave it to slow-cook; it was ready when we got home. We all loved lamb, and she often slow-cooked a leg of lamb when she could get it. We didn't often have dessert at the table any other time than Sunday. My mother made pound cakes a lot (mostly plain vanilla), and we'd have seasonal things like strawberry shortcake, but the thing I remember were those tall banana puddings, layered with homemade custard and vanilla wafers and topped with a golden-brown meringue. Our meals were always casual during the week, but on Sunday we put more effort into the table. How the table was set was a contest: If I got home first, it was laid with my mother's wedding china and silver; if Mama got there first, it was the second-best china and maybe the silver; if one of my brothers or Dad made it home ahead of me, it was the brown stoneware and everyday stainless, but the table was laid with more care.

WHAT DISH DID YOU LOOK FORWARD TO HAVING?

Probably that pot roast: Mama put it on a bed of sliced onions, then smothered it with more, and surrounded it with carrots, celery, and potatoes. The seasonings were Worcestershire, salt, and pepper.

TELL US ABOUT YOUR FAVORITE SUNDAY SUPPER—PAST OR PRESENT.

Since we didn't have a cooked supper (not even a casserole), and often had cold cereal with milk, I guess my favorite would be the times when we had leftover roast cold, especially when it was leg of lamb. My older brother would concoct a barbecue sauce with a handful of condiments, and we'd eat the meat cold with the sauce or use it to make sandwiches.

This chicken and dumplings will make your heart sing. It's the kind of recipe that takes the chill off an inclement day. Whether you're sitting by the fire or gathered at the table, the warmth will fill your tummy and make you smile.

Start this dish early, allowing plenty of time for straining and reducing the broth and for making the sweet potato dumplings. The simple salad requires only a little extra time to toast the walnuts. The dressing can be made earlier in the day. Rum punch is a treat, a bright spot on a gloomy day. Assemble the punch just before serving.

Chicken and Sweet Potato
DUMPLINGS

Serves 8   Hands-on 1 hour   Total 6 hours, 25 minutes, including dumplings

2 medium-size baking potatoes (about ¾ pound)
1 large sweet potato (about ½ pound)
1 (3 ¾-pound) whole chicken
2 celery ribs, chopped
2 carrots, chopped
1 medium onion, quartered
4 garlic cloves, crushed
3 fresh thyme sprigs
1 ½ teaspoons kosher salt
½ teaspoon freshly ground black pepper
¼ cup freshly grated Parmesan cheese
1 large egg
½ teaspoon chopped fresh rosemary
¼ teaspoon kosher salt
¼ teaspoon freshly ground black pepper
½ cup all-purpose flour
½ medium onion, thinly sliced
2 carrots, sliced
1 celery rib, thinly sliced
Shaved Parmesan cheese
Flat-leaf parsley leaves

1. Preheat oven to 400°F. Prick all potatoes with a fork, and bake on a jelly-roll pan 1 hour.

2. Bring chicken, next 7 ingredients, and water to cover to a boil in a Dutch oven over medium heat. Cover, reduce heat to medium-low; simmer 1 hour.

3. Remove chicken, reserving broth. Remove potatoes, and set aside. Cool chicken and potatoes 30 minutes until cool enough to handle. Simmer reserved broth in the Dutch oven over low heat 30 minutes while chicken and potatoes cool.

4. Skin, bone, and shred chicken, reserving bones. Place bones in broth. Cover and chill shredded chicken until ready to use. Cook broth, uncovered, over low heat 1 hour or until reduced by one-third.

5. While broth reduces, peel and mash potatoes until smooth. Add cheese and next 4 ingredients; stir until smooth. Fold in flour just until blended. Divide dough into 4 equal portions; dust with flour. Roll each into a ¾-inch-diameter rope on a well-floured surface. Cut into 1-inch pieces; place on a floured baking sheet.

6. Strain broth into a bowl; discard solids. Wipe Dutch oven clean; pour broth back into Dutch oven. Skim fat from broth. Add the onion and next 2 ingredients to broth; cook over medium-high heat, 20 minutes or until carrots are crisp-tender. Add shredded chicken; return to a simmer.

7. Cook dumplings, 10 to 12 at a time, in 3 quarts boiling water over medium-high heat 3 minutes. Remove with a slotted spoon.

8. Add dumplings to soup. Sprinkle with Parmesan and parsley; serve immediately.

Easy
ROMAINE TOSS

Serves 8   Hands-on 10 minutes   Total 10 minutes

⅓ cup sherry vinegar
¼ cup balsamic vinegar
2 teaspoons Dijon mustard
1 garlic clove, minced
½ teaspoon salt
¼ teaspoon coarsely ground black pepper
½ cup walnut oil*
½ cup olive oil
8 cups torn romaine lettuce or mixed salad greens
Toasted walnuts (optional)
Tomato wedges (optional)

Process first 6 ingredients in a blender or food processor until smooth. Turn blender on high; add oils in a slow, steady stream. Chill, if desired. Serve dressing at room temperature with lettuce and, if desired, toasted walnuts and tomato wedges.

*½ cup olive oil may be substituted.

To toast the walnuts, heat in a small nonstick skillet over medium–low heat, stirring often, about 6 to 8 minutes or until toasted and fragrant.

Sparkling RUM PUNCH

Makes about 9 cups   *Hands-on 10 minutes*
Total 1 hour, 10 minutes

2 cups fresh orange juice
½ cup orange liqueur
½ cup dark rum
2 (750-milliliter) bottles sparkling wine, chilled
Rosemary sprig (optional)
Orange slice (optional)

Stir together orange juice, orange liqueur, and rum in a
medium bowl; cover and chill 1 hour. Pour mixture into a
large pitcher or punch bowl, and top with chilled sparkling
wine. Serve immediately.

MENU THREE

SERVES 6-8

**SPRING CHICKEN
RISOTTO** (page 135)

**EASY THREE-SEED
PAN ROLLS** (page 136)

**CARAMEL-MOCHA-SEA
SALT CUPCAKES** (page 137)

Risotto is a creamy rice dish made with Arborio rice, an Italian short-grain rice containing a higher starch content than long-grain rice. This starch helps to yield the signature creamy texture of risotto. The chicken and vegetables are cooked separately from the rice so as not to interfere with the absorption of the broth by the rice. The pan rolls get a jump-start with frozen bread dough rolls, but the fennel, poppy, and sesame seeds add from-scratch flavor. The caramel-mocha-sea salt combination is pure, rich decadence for dessert.

Plan ahead to allow the rolls to rise three to four hours and be popped in a hot oven as the risotto finishes. The cupcakes can be made a day ahead, or earlier the same day, and kept in the refrigerator. Remove and bring to room temperature before sitting down to supper. The risotto is a hands-on dish, so pour a glass of wine and enjoy the rhythm of the stirring and adding of the broth. The chicken and vegetables are cooked before the risotto so nothing disturbs the process.

Spring Chicken
RISOTTO

Serves 6 to 8　　*Hands-on 1 hour, 15 minutes*　　*Total 1 hour, 15 minutes*

4 cups chicken broth
½ pound fresh asparagus spears
¾ pound skinned and boned chicken breasts, cut into 1-inch strips
½ teaspoon herbes de Provence, fennel seeds, rosemary, or thyme
1¼ teaspoons salt
3 tablespoons butter
2 tablespoons olive oil
2 medium zucchini, thinly sliced into half moons
1 medium onion, finely chopped
2½ cups uncooked Arborio rice (short-grain)
1 cup dry white wine
1 cup freshly grated Parmesan cheese
½ cup freshly grated fontina cheese
¼ cup chopped fresh parsley
½ teaspoon freshly ground black pepper

1. Bring chicken broth and 4 cups water to a simmer in a large saucepan over low heat. Snap off and discard tough ends of asparagus. Cut into 2-inch pieces. Sprinkle chicken with herbes de Provence and ¾ teaspoon salt.

2. Melt 2 tablespoons butter with 1 tablespoon olive oil in a Dutch oven over medium-high heat; add chicken, and sauté 5 to 6 minutes or until done. Remove chicken; cover and keep warm.

3. Melt remaining 1 tablespoon butter in Dutch oven; add zucchini, onion, and asparagus, and sauté 3 minutes or until tender. Remove vegetables; cover and keep warm.

4. Sauté rice in remaining 1 tablespoon hot oil in Dutch oven over medium-high heat 1 minute. Reduce heat to medium. Add wine and remaining ½ teaspoon salt, and cook, stirring often, until liquid is absorbed. Add 1 cup hot broth mixture; cook, stirring often, until liquid is absorbed. Repeat procedure with remaining broth mixture, 1 cup at a time. (Total cooking time is about 30 minutes.) Stir in grated cheeses, chicken, and vegetables until creamy. Stir in parsley and pepper. Serve immediately.

Easy Three-Seed
PAN ROLLS

Makes 9 rolls *Hands-on 10 minutes*
Total 3 hours, 25 minutes

4 teaspoons fennel seeds
4 teaspoons poppy seeds
4 teaspoons sesame seeds
9 frozen bread dough rolls
1 egg white, beaten
Melted butter

1. Combine first 3 ingredients in a small bowl. Dip dough rolls, 1 at a time, in egg white; roll in seed mixture. Arrange rolls, 1 inch apart, in a lightly greased 8-inch pan. Cover with lightly greased plastic wrap, and let rise in a warm place (85°F), free from drafts, 3 to 4 hours or until doubled in bulk.

2. Preheat the oven to 350°F. Uncover rolls, and bake at 350°F for 15 minutes or until golden. Brush with melted butter.

Variation

THREE-SEED FRENCH BREAD:
Substitute 1 (11-ounce) can refrigerated French bread dough for frozen bread dough rolls. Combine seeds in a shallow dish. Brush dough loaf with egg white. Roll top and sides of dough loaf in seeds. Place, seam side down, on a baking sheet. Cut and bake dough loaf according to package directions.

Caramel-Mocha-Sea Salt
CUPCAKES

Makes 24 cupcakes *Hands-on 40 minutes*
Total 1 hour, 24 minutes

CHOCOLATE CAKE
1 cup Dutch process cocoa
2 cups boiling water
1 cup butter, softened
2 cups superfine sugar
4 large eggs
2 ¾ cups all-purpose soft-wheat
   flour
1 teaspoon baking soda
1 teaspoon baking powder
½ teaspoon salt
1 teaspoon chocolate extract
Paper baking cups
Vegetable cooking spray

MOCHA FROSTING
1 cup butter, softened
¾ cup unsweetened cocoa
½ teaspoon salt
2 teaspoons coffee extract
2 (16-ounce) packages powdered
   sugar
⅓ cup whipping cream

Caramel Drizzle

TOPPINGS
Coarse sea salt
Candy espresso beans

1. To prepare cake, preheat oven to 350°F. Combine cocoa and 2 cups boiling water in a large heatproof bowl, stirring until blended and smooth; cool completely. Beat butter at medium speed with an electric mixer until creamy; gradually add sugar, beating until blended. Add eggs, 1 at a time, beating until blended after each addition. Combine flour and next 3 ingredients; add to butter mixture alternately with cocoa mixture, beginning and ending with flour mixture. Beat at low speed just until blended after each addition. Stir in chocolate extract.

2. Place paper baking cups in 2 (12-cup) muffin pans, and coat with cooking spray; spoon batter into cups, filling two-thirds full. Bake for 12 to 15 minutes. Cool in pans on wire racks 10 minutes; remove from pans, and cool completely.

3. To prepare frosting, beat first 4 ingredients at medium speed with an electric mixer until creamy. Gradually add powdered sugar alternately with cream, beating at low speed until blended after each addition. Beat at high speed 2 minutes or until creamy.

4. Frost each cupcake with the Mocha Frosting using metal tip no. 12. Drizzle each cupcake with Caramel Drizzle; top each with about ⅛ teaspoon sea salt and 1 espresso bean.

Caramel Drizzle

Cook ½ cup butter and 1 cup sugar in a 2-quart heavy metal saucepan over high heat, stirring occasionally, until mixture is caramel-colored, about 4 to 5 minutes. Remove from heat, and slowly add 1 cup whipping cream, stirring constantly until blended. Return to heat, and bring to a boil; cook 1 to 2 minutes, stirring occasionally. Cool. Makes about 1½ cups.

MENU FOUR
SERVES 6-8

SWEET TEA-BRINED FRIED CHICKEN (page 139)

OLD-FASHIONED SUCCOTASH (page 140)

MOCHA FUDGE COBBLER (page 141)

Fried chicken is a quintessential Sunday dish; this overnight sweet tea-brined chicken fries up extra crispy. The menu says summer in every way with the succotash of lima beans, corn, and chives. Buttermilk biscuits are one of my favorites. Don't be afraid of the wet dough—moisture is crucial to making the steam that produces light and tender layers. The mocha fudge cobbler is a rich finish to this Southern supper.

The succotash can be made ahead and tossed over heat in a skillet just before serving. The biscuits can be cut and refrigerated until time to bake. The cobbler should be made early in the day (or at least before frying the chicken). It can sit at room temperature or be reheated before serving. Frying chicken is considered nearly a spiritual task, so save your attention for this dish.

Sweet Tea-Brined
FRIED CHICKEN

Serves 6 to 8   *Hands-on 30 minutes*   *Total 1 hour, 55 minutes, plus 1 day for marinating*

2 family-size tea bags
½ cup firmly packed light brown sugar
¼ cup kosher salt
1 small sweet onion, thinly sliced
1 lemon, thinly sliced
4 garlic cloves, halved
1 tablespoon cracked black pepper
2 cups ice cubes
1 (3½-pound) cut-up whole chicken
2 cups self-rising flour
1 cup self-rising white cornmeal mix
2 tablespoons freshly ground black pepper
2 teaspoons salt
1 teaspoon ground red pepper
Vegetable oil

1. Bring 4 cups water to a boil in a 3-quart heavy saucepan; add tea bags. Remove from heat; cover and steep 10 minutes. Discard tea bags. Stir in brown sugar and next 5 ingredients, stirring until sugar dissolves. Cool completely (about 45 minutes); stir in ice. (Mixture should be cold before adding to chicken.)

2. Cut chicken breasts in half crosswise. Place tea mixture and all chicken pieces in a large zip-top plastic freezer bag; seal. Place bag in a shallow baking dish, and chill 24 hours. Remove chicken from marinade, discarding marinade. Drain chicken well.

3. Whisk together flour and next 4 ingredients in a medium bowl. Spoon 1 cup flour mixture into a brown paper bag or large zip-top plastic freezer bag. Place 1 piece of chicken in bag; seal and shake to coat. Remove chicken, and transfer to a wire rack. Repeat procedure with remaining chicken, adding more flour mixture to bag as needed. Let chicken stand 30 minutes to form a crust.

4. Pour oil to depth of 1½ inches into a cast-iron Dutch oven (or 1 inch in a 12-inch skillet); heat over medium heat to 325°F. Fry chicken, in batches, 15 to 22 minutes or until browned and done, turning occasionally. Drain on a wire rack over paper towels.

Old-Fashioned
SUCCOTASH

Serves 6   *Hands-on 40 minutes*   *Total 40 minutes*

2 cups fresh lima beans
4 fresh thyme sprigs
½ small onion
1 garlic clove
1½ cups diced sweet onion
2 tablespoons olive oil
4 cups fresh corn kernels (about 6 ears)
1 teaspoon honey
2 tablespoons unsalted butter
3 tablespoons chopped fresh chives

1. Place lima beans, thyme sprigs, onion half, and garlic in a medium saucepan, and cover with water. Bring mixture to a boil over medium-high heat; reduce heat to medium, and simmer, stirring occasionally, 20 minutes or until beans are tender. Drain beans, reserving ½ cup cooking liquid. Discard thyme sprigs, onion, and garlic.

2. Sauté diced onion in hot oil in a large skillet over medium-high heat 5 minutes. Stir in corn and honey; cook, stirring often, 6 minutes or until corn is tender. Stir in beans and ½ cup reserved cooking liquid; cook, stirring occasionally, 5 minutes. Stir in butter, and add salt and pepper to taste. Sprinkle with chives.

Mocha Fudge
COBBLER

Serves 8 to 10   *Hands-on 10 minutes*
Total 1 hour, 10 minutes

1 cup all-purpose flour
2 teaspoons baking powder
¼ teaspoon salt
1¼ cups granulated sugar
¼ cup plus 2 tablespoons unsweetened cocoa
½ cup milk
⅓ cup vegetable oil
1 teaspoon vanilla extract
½ cup firmly packed light brown sugar
1½ cups hot brewed coffee
Whipped cream or ice cream (optional)

1. Preheat oven to 350°F. Stir together first 3 ingredients, ¾ cup granulated sugar, and 2 tablespoons cocoa in a medium bowl. Stir together milk, oil, and vanilla; add to flour mixture, stirring until dry ingredients are moistened. Spread batter into a lightly greased 2-quart baking dish.

2. Stir together brown sugar, remaining ½ cup granulated sugar, and remaining ¼ cup cocoa in a small bowl; sprinkle over batter in pan. Using a spoon, gently drizzle hot coffee over brown sugar mixture, being careful not to disturb layers. (Do not stir.)

3. Bake at 350°F for 35 to 40 minutes or until a cake layer forms on top and springs back when lightly touched. Remove from oven to a wire rack, and cool 25 minutes. Serve warm with whipped cream or ice cream, if desired.

MENU FIVE

SERVES 6-8

**DOUBLE-CRUST
CHICKEN POT PIE** (PAGE 143)

**WALDORF SPINACH
SALAD** (PAGE 144)

**FRESH APPLE
CAKE** (PAGE 145)

Puff pastry makes a lovely dough for chicken pot pie, and this recipe uses both a top and bottom crust for extra goodness. The leeks make this pie one of my favorites, but onions or shallots may be substituted if desired. Chock-full of chicken and vegetables, this is a rib-sticking dose of home comfort. Our Waldorf salad is quick to make and lighter than the traditional version. All the expected ingredients are there—apples, celery, nuts, and raisins—and the bed of spinach leaves gives the salad a modern flair. A cinnamon-kissed vinaigrette replaces the usual mayonnaise. The apple theme continues with a dessert of fresh apple cake with a browned-butter frosting. Need I say more?

Defrost the puff pastry, still in its package, on the counter about 30 minutes before needed. If no cooked chicken is on hand, sauté chicken breasts while the pastry defrosts. The salad comes together quickly near the end of the cooking time for the chicken. Dress the salad just before serving to prevent the leaves from becoming soggy. The apple cake can be made up to a day ahead and refrigerated, removing just before supper to come to room temperature before serving.

Double-Crust CHICKEN POT PIE

Serves 6 to 8   *Hands-on 30 minutes*   *Total 1 hour, 40 minutes*

½ cup butter
2 medium-size leeks, rinsed and sliced
½ cup all-purpose flour
1 (14.5-ounce) can chicken broth
3 cups chopped cooked chicken
1½ cups frozen cubed hash browns with onions and peppers
1 cup matchstick carrots
⅓ cup chopped fresh flat-leaf parsley
½ teaspoon salt
½ teaspoon freshly ground black pepper
1 (17.3-ounce) package frozen puff pastry sheets, thawed
1 large egg
1 tablespoon water

1. Preheat oven to 375°F. Melt butter in a large skillet over medium heat; add leeks, and sauté 3 minutes. Sprinkle with flour; cook, stirring constantly, 3 minutes. Whisk in chicken broth; bring to a boil, whisking constantly. Remove from heat; stir in chicken and next 5 ingredients.

2. Roll each pastry sheet into a 12- x 10-inch rectangle on a lightly floured surface. Fit 1 sheet into a 9-inch deep-dish pie plate; spoon chicken mixture into pastry. Place remaining pastry sheet over filling in opposite direction of bottom sheet; fold edges under, and press with tines of a fork, sealing to bottom crust. Whisk together egg and 1 tablespoon water, and brush over top of pie.

3. Bake at 375°F on lower oven rack 55 to 60 minutes or until browned. Let stand 15 minutes.

Waldorf Spinach
SALAD

Serves 6   *Hands-on 25 minutes*   *Total 25 minutes*

¼ cup honey
3 tablespoons vegetable oil
2 tablespoons cider vinegar
½ teaspoon dry mustard
¼ teaspoon ground cinnamon
1 garlic clove, pressed
⅛ teaspoon salt
1 (9-ounce) package fresh spinach, torn
2 large Gala apples, thinly sliced
4 ounces extra-sharp white Cheddar cheese, shaved
1 cup thinly sliced celery
1 cup honey-roasted cashews
½ cup golden raisins

Whisk together first 7 ingredients in a large serving bowl until well blended. Add spinach and remaining ingredients, tossing gently to coat. Serve immediately.

Fresh
APPLE CAKE

Serves 12 to 15   Hands-on 30 minutes
Total 3 hours, 20 minutes, including frosting

½ cup butter, melted
2 cups sugar
2 large eggs
1 teaspoon vanilla extract
2 cups all-purpose flour
2 teaspoons ground cinnamon
1 teaspoon baking soda

1 teaspoon salt
2½ pounds Granny Smith apples
   (about 4 large), peeled and cut
   into ¼-inch-thick wedges
1½ cups chopped toasted pecans
Vegetable cooking spray
Browned-Butter Frosting

1. Preheat oven to 350°F. Stir together butter and next 3 ingredients in a large bowl until blended.

2. Combine flour and next 3 ingredients; add to butter mixture, stirring until blended. Stir in apples and 1 cup pecans. (Batter will be very thick, similar to a cookie dough.) Lightly grease a 13- x 9-inch pan with cooking spray. Pour batter into pan. Bake at 350°F for 45 minutes or until a wooden pick inserted in center comes out clean. Cool completely in pan on a wire rack (about 45 minutes). Spread Browned-Butter Frosting over top of cake; sprinkle with remaining ½ cup pecans.

Browned-Butter Frosting

Makes about 3½ cups   Hands-on 20 minutes
Total 1 hour, 20 minutes

1 cup butter
1 (16 ounce) package powdered
   sugar

¼ cup milk
1 teaspoon vanilla extract

Cook butter in a small heavy saucepan over medium heat, stirring constantly, 6 to 8 minutes or until butter begins to turn golden brown. Remove pan from heat immediately, and pour butter into a small bowl. Cover and chill 1 hour or until butter is cool and begins to solidify. Beat butter at medium speed with an electric mixer until fluffy; gradually add powdered sugar alternately with milk, beginning and ending with powdered sugar. Beat mixture at low speed until well blended after each addition. Stir in vanilla extract.

MENU SIX

SERVES 6-8

The slow cooker is not only a boon to the weekday cook, it's also a boon to the Sunday cook. These chicken thighs scented with rosemary, garlic, and paprika benefit tremendously from the browning in a skillet before assembling in the slow cooker. The fingerling potatoes absorb flavor from the chicken juices and emerge fork-tender and tasty. The Beet-and-Citrus Salad deliciously balances sweet and tart. If you prefer, substitute other citrus fruits such as tangelos, blood oranges, or clementines for the grapefruit. The Hot Toddy is a bold and warm whiskey drink that begs to be enjoyed fireside.

Plan ahead to allow for the browning of the chicken and the four hours of slow-cooking time, and note that the potatoes are added halfway through the cooking time. The beets bake for one hour; to avoid staining, use rubber gloves and a plastic cutting board when handling the beets. The Hot Toddy can be preset and ready for the boiling water just before serving.

ROSEMARY-GARLIC CHICKEN QUARTERS (page 148)

BEET-AND-CITRUS SALAD (page 151)

HOT TODDY (page 152)

SET THE
SCENE

Setting a festive table outdoors is fun nearly year-round in the South.

Tablescapes is the word used to define what is decoratively set on a table. I haul out fabrics, linens, and cloths and use something I haven't used in a while. It's fun to see some of my favorites that have been pushed to the back of the closet. Will it be a full tablecloth, a table runner, or place mats? That's my starting place. Next I'll choose the table settings—china, casual plates, pottery—whatever seems to suit the menu and the guest list. Finally I'll choose what works for the table. I favor a winding row of votives interlaced with cuttings from shrubs, trees, flowers, or herbs. Fruits and vegetables of the season are always a smart touch, and you can cook with them later.

Fall tablescapes embrace the colors of the season. Here we have gathered slim branches still holding their leaves for a tall centerpiece. The branches should be tall enough not to encroach on the line of sight across the table. Simple votive candles in carved-out miniature pumpkins work well as candleholders, or use the pumpkins as place cards.

We selected a menu that is easy on the cook—you'll run in and out of doors less. Set up lawn games such as horseshoes or croquet for some old-fashioned fun—adults love to have a chance to revisit their childhood. As the night cools down, light a patio fire pit and gather round to extend the evening.

Rosemary – Garlic
CHICKEN QUARTERS

Serves 6 to 8   Hands-on 25 minutes   Total 4 hours, 25 minutes

3 carrots or celery ribs
5 pounds chicken leg quarters
2 tablespoons chopped fresh rosemary
2 teaspoons pimentón (sweet smoked Spanish paprika)
2 ½ teaspoons kosher salt
1 ¼ teaspoons freshly ground black pepper
12 garlic cloves, sliced
3 tablespoons olive oil
½ cup chicken broth
2 pounds fingerling Yukon gold potatoes, halved lengthwise
1 teaspoon olive oil

1. Place carrots in a single layer in a 5-quart slow cooker.

2. Remove skin from chicken, and trim fat. Stir together rosemary, pimentón, 1½ teaspoons salt, and 1 teaspoon pepper. Rub mixture over chicken.

3. Sauté garlic in 3 tablespoons hot oil in a large skillet over medium heat 2 minutes or until golden brown. Transfer to a bowl using a slotted spoon; reserve oil in skillet. Cook half of chicken in reserved oil in skillet 3 to 4 minutes on each side or until deep golden brown. Transfer to slow cooker, reserving drippings in skillet. Repeat with remaining chicken.

4. Add broth and garlic to reserved drippings in skillet, and cook 1 minute, stirring to loosen particles from bottom of skillet; pour over chicken in slow cooker. Cover and cook on HIGH 2 hours.

5. Toss potatoes with 1 teaspoon oil and remaining 1 teaspoon salt and ¼ teaspoon pepper; add to slow cooker. Cover and cook 2 more hours.

6. Transfer chicken and potatoes to a serving platter, and pour juices from slow cooker through a fine wire-mesh strainer into a bowl; skim fat from juices. Serve immediately with chicken and potatoes.

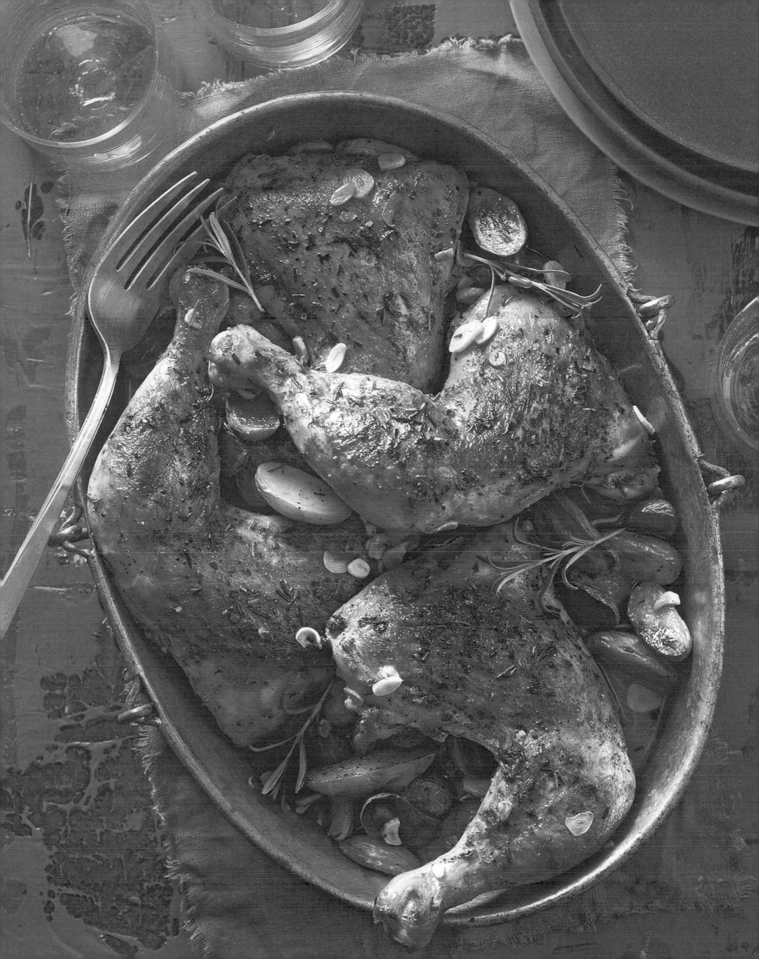

Beet-and-Citrus
SALAD

Serves 8 to 10   *Hands-on 30 minutes*   *Total 2 hours, 10 minutes*

3 medium-size fresh beets
3 Ruby Red grapefruit
¼ cup olive oil
2 tablespoons maple syrup
2 tablespoons white wine vinegar
1 teaspoon kosher salt
¼ teaspoon freshly ground black pepper
6 cups loosely packed arugula
¼ cup coarsely chopped pistachios

1. Preheat oven to 350°F. Trim beet stems to 1 inch; gently wash beets, and place in an 8-inch square pan. Add ¼ cup water, and cover with aluminum foil. Bake 1 hour and 10 minutes or until tender. Uncover and cool completely (about 30 minutes).

2. Cut a ¼-inch-thick slice from each end of grapefruit using a sharp, thin-bladed knife. Place, flat ends down, on a cutting board, and remove peel in strips, cutting from top to bottom following the curvature of fruit. Remove any remaining bitter white pith. Holding peeled grapefruit over a bowl, slice between membranes, and gently remove whole segments. Reserve ¼ cup juice.

3. Whisk together olive oil, next 4 ingredients, and reserved ¼ cup grapefruit juice in a bowl.

4. Peel beets, and slice into wedges. Arrange arugula on a large platter; top with grapefruit and beets. Drizzle with vinaigrette; sprinkle with pistachios. Add salt and pepper to taste.

Hot TODDY

Serves 1   *Hands-on 10 minutes*
Total 55 minutes, including Simple Syrup

8 whole cloves
8 raisins
2 ounces rye whiskey
½ ounce Simple Syrup

Pinch of nutmeg
1 ounce boiling water
1 cinnamon stick

Insert cloves into raisins. Place in a heat-proof glass. Stir together rye whiskey, Simple Syrup, and nutmeg until blended; pour over raisins. Add 1 ounce boiling water. Stir gently using a cinnamon stick, and let stand 10 minutes. Serve as is, or pour into a brandy snifter.

To serve 8, set 8 glasses on a tray and distribute 8 clove-speared raisins in each glass. Combine 2 cups rye whiskey with 1 cup Simple Syrup and ½ teaspoon nutmeg. Divide among glasses. Pour 1 ounce boiling water in each cup, stir with cinnamon stick, and let stand 10 minutes before serving.

Simple Syrup

Bring 1 cup water and 1 cup sugar to a boil in a small saucepan, stirring until sugar dissolves; boil 1 minute. Remove from heat, and let cool 30 minutes. Makes 2 cups.

SOUTHERN SAVVY
THE ART OF TOASTING

There's hardly a reason not to toast at a gathering, plus it puts everyone in a festive mood! Other than at weddings, there are no rigid rules to follow for toasting. And although we may most associate toasting with wine, any beverage is appropriate. Even if there is not a special occasion for the gathering, and even if it is just a casual poolside get-together, the host is encouraged to greet the guests in a welcome toast—to the day, to their health, to a piece of good news. The most helpful bit of toasting advice is for the guests: Delay drinking from your glass until your host either gives the toast or drinks from his glass without toasting, signaling there won't be a toast. If you happen to be the recipient of the toast, just nod and smile to indicate your delight. You may return with a toast of your own, or not. Cheers!

SUNDAYS PAST & PRESENT
with KENDRA BAILEY MORRIS

Meet Kendra Bailey Morris, author of *The Southern Slow Cooker: Big-Flavor, Low-Fuss Recipes for Comfort Food Classics.*
HOMETOWN: Morgantown, WV **RESIDES:** Richmond, VA

WHAT COMES TO MIND WHEN YOU THINK OF MEALS FROM SUNDAYS PAST?

For me, the beauty of the Sunday supper is that you can always rely on it. I grew up in the Southern Baptist church, and as you may know, Southern Baptists love to eat. Every Sunday after church service, without fail, we'd gather at the table as a family. Sometimes we'd cook a big country-style meal, other times we'd nosh something quick like pimiento cheese sandwiches. On special occasions, our church would have a big potluck outside on the grounds. Those were always the best, not only because you could eat your fill of fried chicken and biscuits, but you could pile your plate with banana pudding, lemon pound cake, and chocolate chess pie and no one would judge you for it. I always enjoyed this Sunday afternoon fellowship.

WHAT DISH DID YOU LOOK FORWARD TO HAVING?

What dish *didn't* I look forward to, you mean? It's hard to pick just one, but if I had to choose, I'd go with my mom's Circle Salad, a gelatin concoction made with lemon gelatin, cream cheese, whipped cream, pimientos, and pecans. It's a dish that originated from our church Bible study group, also known as the Women's Circle Group. The recipe sounds like a strange combination, but, trust me, it's absolutely delicious!

TELL US ABOUT YOUR FAVORITE SUNDAY SUPPER—PAST OR PRESENT.

My favorite memories are of my granny's suppers that she used to cook for the family back in West Virginia. She would cook for days on end, filling two refrigerators with baked ham, homemade rolls, cream gravy, pole beans from her garden, pinto beans cooked in fatback, gritted cornbread, and skillet-fried apples from her backyard apple tree. There was so much food that we couldn't fit it all on one table, so during the winter months, Granny would store half of it out on the back porch. We'd talk and eat for hours. It was such a wonderful time. My granny passed away a few years ago, but before she died, she gave me her recipe box. Now, I make her recipes for Sunday supper, and I even store some of the food out on my back porch, just like she did.

This chunky chicken-and-brisket stew is easy to pull together, and most of the cooking is unattended. It's teeming with tomatoes, corn, and lima beans—all classic Brunswick stew ingredients. Cornbread is the traditional side dish, but I've changed it up a bit with sweet potatoes in the mix. The decadent ice-cream cake is truly a mint chocolate lover's dream! The layering of mint chocolate chip ice cream and devil's food chocolate cake with a rich chocolate ganache and chopped crème de menthe chocolate mints becomes the most decadent of desserts.

It's best to make the whole ice-cream cake a day ahead and freeze until ready to serve. The stew can be made ahead and reheated before serving, or plan ahead for the two hours of cooking time. The cornbread is at its best hot out of the oven just before sitting down to supper.

Chicken-and-Brisket
BRUNSWICK STEW

Makes 16 cups   *Hands-on 25 minutes*   *Total 2 hours, 35 minutes*

2 large onions, chopped
2 garlic cloves, minced
1 tablespoon vegetable oil
1½ tablespoons jarred beef soup base
2 pounds uncooked skinned and boned chicken breasts
1 (28-ounce) can fire-roasted crushed tomatoes
1 (12-ounce) package frozen white shoepeg or
   whole kernel corn
1 (10-ounce) package frozen cream-style corn, thawed
1 (9-ounce) package frozen baby lima beans
1 (12-ounce) bottle chili sauce
1 tablespoon brown sugar
1 tablespoon yellow mustard
1 tablespoon Worcestershire sauce
½ teaspoon coarsely ground black pepper
1 pound cooked chopped barbecued beef brisket
   (without sauce)
1 tablespoon fresh lemon juice
Hot sauce (optional)

1. Sauté onions and garlic in hot oil in a 7.5-quart Dutch oven over medium-high heat 3 to 5 minutes or until tender.

2. Stir together beef soup base and 2 cups water, and add to Dutch oven. Stir in chicken and next 9 ingredients. Bring to a boil. Cover, reduce heat to low, and cook, stirring occasionally, 2 hours.

3. Uncover and shred chicken into large pieces using 2 forks. Stir in brisket and lemon juice. Cover and cook 10 minutes. Serve with hot sauce, if desired.

Sweet Potato
CORNBREAD

Serves 6   *Hands-on 15 minutes*   *Total 50 minutes*

2 cups self-rising white cornmeal mix
3 tablespoons sugar
¼ teaspoon pumpkin pie spice
5 large eggs
2 cups cooked mashed sweet potatoes
   (about 1½ pounds sweet potatoes)
1 (8-ounce) container sour cream
½ cup butter, melted

1. Preheat oven to 425°F. Stir together first 3 ingredients in a large bowl; make a well in center of mixture. Whisk together eggs and next 3 ingredients; add to cornmeal mixture, stirring just until moistened. Spoon batter into a lightly greased 9-inch square pan.

2. Bake at 425°F for 35 minutes or until golden brown.

Mint Chocolate Chip
ICE-CREAM CAKE

Serves 10 to 12   Hands-on 30 minutes
Total 10 hours, 7 minutes, including cake batter and ganache

DEVIL'S FOOD CAKE BATTER
Parchment paper
½ cup butter, softened
¾ cup sugar
1 large egg
1 teaspoon vanilla extract
1 cup all-purpose flour
⅓ cup unsweetened cocoa
1 teaspoon baking soda
¾ cup hot strong brewed coffee
1 teaspoon white vinegar

½ gallon mint chocolate chip
  ice cream, softened
10 chocolate wafers, coarsely
  crushed
Chocolate Ganache
Sweetened whipped cream
  (optional)
Thin crème de menthe chocolate
  mints (optional)

1. Preheat oven to 350°F. Grease and flour 3 (8-inch) round cake pans. Line with parchment paper.

2. To prepare Devil's Food Cake Batter, beat butter and sugar at medium speed with a heavy-duty electric stand mixer until creamy. Add egg, beating just until blended. Beat in vanilla. Combine flour, cocoa, and baking soda. Add to butter mixture alternately with coffee, beating until blended. Stir in vinegar. Spoon batter into pans. Bake at 350°F for 12 to 14 minutes or until a wooden pick inserted in center comes out clean. Cool in pans on a wire rack 10 minutes. Remove from pans to wire racks, peel off parchment paper, and cool completely (about 1 hour).

3. Place 1 cake layer in a 9-inch springform pan. Top with one-third of ice cream (about 2⅓ cups); sprinkle with half of crushed wafers. Repeat layers once. Top with remaining cake layer and ice cream. Freeze 8 to 12 hours.

4. Remove cake from springform pan, and place on a cake stand or plate. Prepare Chocolate Ganache, and spread over top of ice-cream cake. Let stand 15 minutes before serving. Top with sweetened whipped cream and crème de menthe chocolate mints, if desired.

Chocolate Ganache

Microwave 1 (4-ounce) chopped semisweet chocolate baking bar and 4 tablespoons whipping cream in a microwave-safe bowl at HIGH 1 minute or until melted, stirring at 30-second intervals. Stir in up to 4 tablespoons additional cream for desired consistency.

MENU EIGHT

SERVES 8

BEER-BATTERED FRIED FISH (PAGE 159)

HUSH PUPPIES (PAGE 160)

CENTRAL TEXAS SLAW (PAGE 161)

Sunday supper is a great time for a fish fry! These grouper fillets are doused in a beer batter before frying and emerge moist and flaky with a lovely coating. No grouper? Substitute any white, flaky fish. The Buttermilk-Ranch-Herb Sauce adds great flavor to the fish. No fish fry is complete without fresh, hot hush puppies. The Central Texas Slaw packs a bit of punch with a Southwestern flair thanks to jalapeño pepper and cilantro.

Assemble the slaw early in the day to allow flavors to meld and the slaw to chill. I love my slaw icy cold. Prepare the hush puppies first and keep on a wire rack in a jelly-roll pan in a 200°F oven. Proceed to frying the fish in batches, keeping the fried fish warm along with the hush puppies. The sauce can be made a day or two ahead and refrigerated.

Beer-Battered FRIED FISH

Serves 8   *Hands-on 30 minutes*   *Total 30 minutes*

Vegetable oil
2 pounds grouper fillets, cut into pieces
2 teaspoons salt
½ teaspoon freshly ground black pepper
1½ cups all-purpose flour
1½ teaspoons sugar
1 (12-ounce) bottle beer
1 teaspoon hot sauce

1. Pour oil to depth of 3 inches into a large Dutch oven; heat to 360°F. Meanwhile, sprinkle fish with 1 teaspoon salt and pepper.

2. Whisk together flour, sugar, and remaining teaspoon salt in a large bowl. Whisk in beer and hot sauce. Dip fish in batter, allowing excess batter to drip off.

3. Gently lower fish into hot oil using tongs (to prevent fish from sticking to Dutch oven). Fry fish, in 4 batches, 2 to 3 minutes on each side or until golden brown. Place fried fish on a wire rack in a jelly-roll pan; keep warm in a 200°F oven until ready to serve.

Buttermilk-Ranch-Herb Sauce

Makes 1⅓ cups   *Hands-on 6 minutes*   *Total 6 minutes*

1 cup mayonnaise
⅓ cup buttermilk
1½ tablespoons chopped fresh chives
2 teaspoons Ranch dressing mix
1 teaspoon lemon zest
3 tablespoons fresh lemon juice
½ teaspoon freshly ground black pepper
¼ teaspoon salt

Whisk together mayonnaise, buttermilk, chives, Ranch dressing mix, lemon zest, fresh lemon juice, freshly ground pepper, and salt. Serve immediately, or cover and chill up to 2 days.

HUSH PUPPIES

Serves 8 to 10 (about 2 dozen)   *Hands-on 25 minutes*
Total 35 minutes

Vegetable oil
1½ cups self-rising white cornmeal mix
¾ cup self-rising flour
¾ cup diced sweet onion (about ½ medium onion)
1½ tablespoons sugar
1 large egg, lightly beaten
1¼ cups buttermilk

1. Pour oil to depth of 3 inches into a Dutch oven; heat to 375°F. Combine cornmeal mix and next 3 ingredients. Add egg and buttermilk; stir just until moistened. Let stand 10 minutes.

2. Drop batter by rounded tablespoonfuls into hot oil, and fry, in 3 batches, 2 to 3 minutes on each side or until golden. Drain on paper towels. Place on a wire rack in a jelly-roll pan, and keep warm in a 200°F oven.

Stir hush puppy batter just until moistened. Overmixing causes them to be tough.

Central Texas
SLAW

Makes about 4 cups   *Hands-on 15 minutes*
Total 1 hour, 15 minutes

¼ cup white vinegar
¼ cup extra virgin olive oil
2 tablespoons sugar
3 to 4 tablespoons fresh lime juice
1½ teaspoons kosher salt
½ teaspoon ground coriander
¼ teaspoon ground cumin
¼ teaspoon ground red pepper
¼ teaspoon freshly ground black pepper
2 cups thinly sliced red cabbage
2 cups thinly sliced white cabbage
½ cup shredded carrot
1 medium jalapeño pepper (with seeds), thinly sliced
½ red bell pepper, thinly sliced
½ yellow bell pepper, thinly sliced
½ cup chopped fresh cilantro

Whisk together vinegar, olive oil, sugar, lime juice, kosher salt, ground coriander, ground cumin, ground red pepper, and freshly ground black pepper in a large bowl. Add red cabbage, white cabbage, carrot, jalapeño pepper, red bell pepper, and yellow bell pepper. Toss to coat. Chill 1 hour before serving, tossing occasionally. Stir in cilantro just before serving.

MENU NINE

SERVES 8

This rustic stew was inspired by the rich, meaty flavors of a crawfish or shrimp boil and is brimming with sausage, peppers, potatoes, fish fillets, shrimp, and crawfish tails. Substitute more shrimp for the crawfish, if desired. The corn cakes are perfect for dunking in the heavenly stew broth. Pear-and-Blue Cheese Crostini with a bit of chopped bacon and arugula keep hunger at bay. The crostini can be prepared a couple of hours in advance. Cook the corn cakes before starting the stew and keep them warm in a 200°F oven until needed. The stew will keep you busy at the beginning and at the end, with about 30 minutes of reprieve in the middle. Have everything at the ready before the stew is done, as it is best served piping hot the minute the shrimp and crawfish are cooked.

GULF COAST
SEAFOOD STEW (page 165)

PEAR-AND-BLUE CHEESE
CROSTINI (page 166)

GRIDDLE
CORN CAKES (page 168)

SET THE
SCENE

When I can get fresh Gulf seafood, I pull out this recipe for a one-pot feast.

For years my sister and I have convened our families on Florida's Gulf coast. It began as a Thanksgiving week reunion, but it moved to winter break as the children reached school age. Our rented three-story vacation home sleeps 18, so we've had extended family and friends share in the pleasures of winter sun with us.

We'll go to town for dinner once during the week. The rest of the time we cook at home and sit together at the giant dining table. It is a special time for all of us as we tell family stories and talk of future plans. We return to the table once it's cleared and enjoy dessert and family game night. Truly these are some of the best memories of my life.

The menu highlight of the week is the seafood stew. We head to the local fish truck where I once purchased the best-tasting grouper I've ever cooked. We'll also pick up some shrimp and add whatever our vacationing fishermen catch that day. For this recipe, use the best shrimp and fish you can afford.

I love serving this stew in deep bowls, and here we have decorated the table with roses cut short in small vases. They make charming place card holders. Layer a rustic linen kitchen towel between a charger and the plate for the place setting—it also catches the drips from the stew. When I make this menu, I am transcended back to our glorious seafood suppers at the beach.

Gulf Coast
SEAFOOD STEW

Serves 8   Hands-on 55 minutes   Total 1 hour, 35 minutes

1½ pounds unpeeled, medium-size raw shrimp
2 celery ribs
1 large sweet onion
2 quarts reduced-sodium fat-free chicken broth
12 ounces andouille sausage, cut into ½-inch pieces
1 poblano pepper, seeded and chopped
1 green bell pepper, chopped
1 tablespoon canola oil
3 garlic cloves, chopped
1 pound small red potatoes, halved
1 (12-ounce) bottle beer
1 tablespoon fresh thyme leaves
2 fresh bay leaves
2 teaspoons Creole seasoning
1½ pounds fresh white fish fillets, (such as snapper, grouper, or catfish), cubed
1 pound cooked crawfish tails (optional)

1. Peel shrimp; place shells in a saucepan. (Refrigerate shrimp until ready to use.) Add celery ends and onion peel to pan; chop remaining celery and onion. (Using the leftover bits of onion and celery will layer the flavor and result in a flavorful broth.) Add broth; bring to a boil over medium-high heat. Reduce heat to low; simmer 30 minutes.

2. Meanwhile, cook sausage in a large Dutch oven over medium-high heat, stirring often, 7 to 8 minutes or until browned. Remove sausage; pat dry. Wipe Dutch oven clean. Sauté celery, onion, poblano pepper, and bell pepper in hot oil in Dutch oven over medium-high heat 5 to 7 minutes or until onion is tender. Add garlic, and sauté 45 seconds to 1 minute or until fragrant. Stir in potatoes, next 4 ingredients, and sausage.

3. Pour broth mixture through a fine wire-mesh strainer into Dutch oven, discarding solids. Increase heat to high, and bring to a boil. Reduce heat to low, and cook, stirring occasionally, 20 to 30 minutes or until potatoes are tender.

4. Add fish; cook 2 to 3 minutes or until just opaque. Add shrimp, and cook 2 to 3 minutes or just until shrimp turn pink. If desired, stir in crawfish, and cook 2 to 3 minutes or until hot. Discard bay leaves. Add salt and pepper to taste.

Pear-and-Blue Cheese
CROSTINI

Serves 8   *Hands-on 5 minutes*   *Total 19 minutes, including Crostini*

1 ripe pear, thinly sliced
Crostini
1 cup firmly packed baby arugula
4 ounces blue cheese, sliced
4 cooked bacon slices, coarsely chopped
Honey

Place 1 pear slice on each Crostini. Top with arugula, cheese, and bacon. Drizzle with honey.

Crostini

Serves 8   *Hands-on 5 minutes*   *Total 14 minutes*

1 (8- to 10-ounce) French bread baguette, cut into
   ½-inch-thick slices (35 to 40 pieces)
2 ½ tablespoons extra virgin olive oil

Preheat oven to 400°F. Place bread in a single layer on a baking sheet, and brush with olive oil. Bake 7 to 8 minutes or until lightly browned. Cool completely on a wire rack (about 2 minutes).

SOUTHERN SAVVY
SEATING

When planning for seating, there is only one seating rule I still oblige. The female guest of honor is seated to the host's right, and the male guest of honor is seated to the hostess's right. The guest of honor can be the eldest at the table, guests from out of town, or the focus of the event, such as when celebrating a newly married couple or wishing friends a bon voyage

Griddle
CORN CAKES

Makes 20 cakes   *Hands-on 10 minutes*   *Total 10 minutes*

2 cups plain white or yellow cornmeal
1 teaspoon kosher salt
1 teaspoon baking soda
1 cup buttermilk
1 large egg, lightly beaten
¼ cup canola oil
1 green onion, thinly sliced
Spiced Mayonnaise

1. Stir together first 3 ingredients in a small bowl.

2. Stir together buttermilk, egg, and 2 tablespoons oil. Stir into cornmeal mixture just until blended. Stir in green onion.

3. Brush 1 tablespoon oil on a hot griddle. Drop cornmeal mixture by ⅛ cupfuls onto hot griddle. Flatten to ½ inch thick, and cook 1½ to 2 minutes on each side or until golden. Repeat process with remaining batter and oil. Serve with Spiced Mayonnaise.

Spiced Mayonnaise

Makes 1 cup   *Hands-on 5 minutes*   *Total 10 minutes*

¼ cup bottled clam juice or chicken broth
Pinch of ground saffron (optional)
1 cup mayonnaise with olive oil (such as Hellmann's with Olive Oil)
2 garlic cloves, minced

Stir together broth and saffron; let stand 5 minutes. Stir together mayonnaise and garlic in a small bowl. Whisk in broth mixture, 2 tablespoons at a time, until smooth and mixture is desired consistency. Serve as a spread for the corn cakes.

SUNDAYS PAST & PRESENT
with JENNIFER HILL BOOKER

Meet Jennifer Hill Booker, author of *Field Peas to Foie Gras: Southern Recipes with a French Accent*, GA Grown executive chef, and owner of Your Resident Gourmet, LLC.

HOMETOWN: Charleston, MS **RESIDES:** Atlanta, GA

WHAT COMES TO MIND WHEN YOU THINK OF MEALS FROM SUNDAYS PAST?

Growing up, Sunday dinner always revolved around family, laughter, delicious smells from the kitchen, and lots of good things to eat! As kids, we knew that there would be a great meal waiting for us when we got home from church, with everything dished up in beautiful platters and bowls. As I grew older, I was allowed to help plan the Sunday dinner menu, shop for ingredients, and even help cook with my mother and grandmother.

WHAT DISH DID YOU LOOK FORWARD TO HAVING?

I come from a family of really great cooks, so all meals were worth looking forward to. But if I had to pick just one that I looked forward to having, I would say that roasted chicken with sage dressing and giblet gravy ranked number one for Sunday dinner favorites. This is followed very closely by pinto beans and smoked ham hocks with buttermilk cornbread!

TELL US ABOUT YOUR FAVORITE SUNDAY SUPPER—PAST OR PRESENT.

When my oldest daughter was a baby, we were stationed at Ft. Lee, Virginia; my baby sister lived in Washington, D.C., and my best friend in Hampton, Virginia. Every Sunday, our families would get together and cook a huge dinner, my favorite being a crab boil. The day before, we drove to the Seafood Wharf in D.C. and bought a bushel of blue crabs, then to the farmers' market for fresh corn, potatoes, andouille sausage, and whatever else looked good to eat. The day of the crab boil, we got up early and cooked all the crabs with the vegetables, sausages, and lots of garlic and onion. Once it was done, we poured everything on a table lined with butcher paper and ate and laughed until we couldn't move. What a wonderful day!

MENU TEN

SERVES 8-10

LOUISIANA GUMBO (PAGE 171)

FIPPS FAMILY POTATO SALAD (PAGE 172)

CARAMEL CAKE (PAGE 173)

Beginning with the holy trinity of Cajun cooking—onion, bell pepper, and celery—this chicken, andouille, and shrimp gumbo is richly flavored and spiced just right. The flour is darkened to a chocolate brown, intensifying the sauce. German settlers introduced potato salads to the region, and in some counties to the west of New Orleans, potato salad is served alongside or even scooped onto the gumbo. Considered a home cook's meal, the combination is rarely seen in restaurants.

Some Sunday suppers call for a beautiful cake to end the day. This Caramel Cake is a guaranteed hit. The cake layers can be made ahead and refrigerated or frozen until needed. The Caramel Frosting is not difficult, but it does require attention. Make sure the cake layers are fully cooled before frosting. The cake can be made and frosted early in the day and left to sit until after Sunday supper.

Prepare all the ingredients ahead for the gumbo. Watch carefully as the flour browns; if it burns, the aroma will tell. If there is a possibility the roux is burned, start over: One can never remove a burned taste from a dish. The potato salad can be made up to a day ahead. If preferred, it can be served warm.

Louisiana
GUMBO

Serves 8 to 10   *Hands-on 40 minutes*   *Total 40 minutes*

½ cup peanut oil
½ cup all-purpose flour
1 cup chopped sweet onion
1 cup chopped green bell pepper
1 cup chopped celery
2 teaspoons Creole seasoning
2 teaspoons minced garlic
3 (14-ounce) cans low-sodium chicken broth
4 cups shredded cooked chicken
½ pound andouille sausage, cut into ¼-inch-thick slices
1½ cups frozen black-eyed peas, thawed
1 pound peeled, jumbo raw shrimp

1. Heat oil in a large Dutch oven over medium-high heat; gradually whisk in flour, and cook, whisking constantly, 5 to 7 minutes or until flour is chocolate colored. (Do not burn mixture.)

2. Reduce heat to medium. Stir in onion and next 4 ingredients, and cook, stirring constantly, 3 minutes. Gradually stir in chicken broth; add chicken and next 2 ingredients. Increase heat to medium-high, and bring to a boil. Reduce heat to low, and simmer, stirring occasionally, 20 minutes. Add shrimp, and cook 5 minutes or just until shrimp turn pink.

Fipps Family
POTATO SALAD

Serves 8 to 10   Hands-on 20 minutes   Total 1 hour

4 pounds baking potatoes (8 large)
3 hard-cooked eggs
1 cup mayonnaise
1 tablespoon Creole or spicy brown mustard
1½ teaspoons salt
¾ teaspoon freshly ground black pepper

1. Cook potatoes in boiling water to cover 40 minutes or until tender; drain and cool. Peel potatoes, and cut into 1-inch cubes.

2. Grate the eggs using the largest holes of a box grater. Stir together potato and egg.

3. Stir together mayonnaise and next 3 ingredients; gently stir into potato mixture. Serve immediately, or cover and chill, if desired.

Eggs that have been refrigerated for a few days are easier to peel than newer eggs.

Caramel
CAKE

Serves 8   Hands-on 15 minutes
Total 3 hours, 35 minutes, including frosting

1 (8-ounce) container sour cream	**CARAMEL FROSTING**
¼ cup milk	⅓ cup sugar
1 cup butter, softened	1 tablespoon all-purpose flour
2 cups sugar	2 ½ cups sugar
4 large eggs	1 cup milk
2 ¾ cups all-purpose flour	¾ cup butter
2 teaspoons baking powder	1 teaspoon vanilla extract
½ teaspoon salt	
1 teaspoon vanilla extract	

1. Preheat oven to 350°F. Combine sour cream and milk. Beat butter at medium speed with an electric mixer until creamy. Gradually add sugar, beating well. Add eggs, 1 at a time, beating until blended after each addition. Combine flour, baking powder, and salt; add to butter mixture alternately with sour cream mixture, beginning and ending with flour mixture. Beat at medium-low speed until blended after each addition. Stir in vanilla. Pour batter into 2 greased and floured 9-inch round cake pans. Bake at 350°F for 30 to 35 minutes or until a wooden pick inserted in center comes out clean. Cool in pans on wire racks 10 minutes. Remove from pans to wire racks, and let cool 1 hour.

2. To prepare Caramel Frosting, sprinkle ⅓ cup sugar in a shallow, heavy 3 ½-quart Dutch oven; cook over medium heat, stirring constantly, 3 minutes or until sugar is melted and syrup is light golden brown (sugar will clump). Remove from heat. Stir together 1 tablespoon flour and 2 ½ cups sugar in a large saucepan; add milk, and bring to a boil over medium-high heat, stirring constantly. Gradually pour about one-fourth hot milk mixture into caramelized sugar, stirring constantly; gradually stir in remaining hot milk mixture until smooth.

3. Cover and cook over low heat 2 minutes. Increase heat to medium; uncover and cook, without stirring, until a candy thermometer reaches 238°F (soft-ball stage; about 10 minutes). Add butter, stirring until blended. Remove from heat and let stand, without stirring, until temperature drops to 110°F (about 1 hour). Pour into bowl of heavy-duty electric stand mixer. Add vanilla, and beat at medium speed with whisk attachment until spreading consistency (about 20 minutes).

4. Spread Caramel Frosting between layers and on top and sides of cake.

A boneless leg of lamb is my go-to dish to impress. It is so easy to prepare, and the aromatic herbs give off an earthy scent while the meat roasts. Set the table with candles and your finest dishes and glassware and prepare for a sparkly evening. The vegetable hash features sweet onions, sweet potatoes, turnips, and Brussels sprouts. Oh—and bacon. Luscious is indeed the word for this lemon cake—three tiers of sweet-tart goodness.

The lamb takes almost three hours from start to finish but only 20 minutes of hands-on time. The vegetable hash is prepared stove-top while the lamb roasts. Substitute carrots for any of the root vegetables, if desired. Make the cake early in the day, cover, and chill until ready to serve. The cake is frosted between the layers and on top. For a more elegant presentation, double the frosting recipe and frost the entire cake.

Herb–Roasted Boneless
LEG OF LAMB

Serves 8 to 10   **Hands-on 20 minutes**   **Total 2 hours, 55 minutes**

1 (5-pound) boneless leg of lamb, rolled and tied
2 teaspoons kosher salt
1 teaspoon freshly ground black pepper
¼ cup loosely packed fresh rosemary leaves
⅔ cup loosely packed fresh flat-leaf parsley leaves
¼ cup loosely packed fresh thyme leaves
2 shallots, coarsely chopped
6 garlic cloves
1 tablespoon fresh lemon juice
6 tablespoons olive oil

1. Rub lamb with 2 teaspoons salt and 1 teaspoon pepper; let stand 1 hour.

2. Pulse rosemary in a food processor 4 or 5 times or until finely chopped. Add parsley and next 4 ingredients, and pulse 4 or 5 times or until finely chopped. Add 6 tablespoons olive oil, and pulse 7 or 8 times or until smooth, scraping down sides as needed. Rub mixture over lamb; place in a large roasting pan. Let stand 30 minutes.

3. Preheat oven to 450°F. Bake for 50 minutes to 1 hour or until a meat thermometer inserted into thickest portion registers 125°F (rare). Remove lamb from pan; cover loosely with aluminum foil, and let stand 15 minutes before slicing. Serve lamb with pan juices.

Note: To roast potatoes with the lamb, toss together 2 pounds small new potatoes and 1½ teaspoons salt, 1 teaspoon freshly ground black pepper, and 4 tablespoons oil; place potatoes around lamb in roasting pan before placing in the preheated oven.

Fall Vegetable
HASH

Serves 8   *Hands-on 35 minutes*   *Total 35 minutes*

4 thick bacon slices
2 tablespoons olive oil
1 medium-size sweet onion, chopped
1 medium-size sweet potato (about 10 ounces), peeled
   and cut into ½-inch cubes
2 medium turnips (about 12 ounces), peeled and cut
   into ½-inch cubes
1 tablespoon white wine vinegar
1 pound small fresh Brussels sprouts, quartered
2 garlic cloves, sliced

1. Cook bacon in a 12-inch cast-iron skillet over medium heat, turning occasionally, 8 to 10 minutes or until crisp. Remove bacon; drain, reserving 2 tablespoons drippings in skillet. Coarsely chop bacon.

2. Add oil to hot drippings in skillet. Cook onion and sweet potato in hot oil and drippings over medium heat, stirring occasionally, 5 minutes. Add turnips; cook, stirring occasionally, 8 minutes.

3. Combine vinegar and 2 tablespoons water. Add Brussels sprouts, garlic, and vinegar mixture to skillet. Cover and cook, stirring occasionally, 5 minutes or until vegetables are tender. Stir in bacon; add salt and pepper to taste.

Emerging succulent and tender, this pulled pork cooks in the slow cooker with just five ingredients. Even if you aren't serving a crowd, let this be your go-to recipe for preparing a big batch of pulled pork for use in sandwiches, wraps, nachos, and more. The Brussels sprouts are simply roasted—I love them when they are roasted at a high heat until the edges begin to lightly brown and the sprouts become tender. Crumbled pancetta takes this side dish over the top, so omit the pancetta if desired. This sinfully rich dessert is perfect blend of fresh bananas, creamy cheesecake, and crunchy vanilla wafers.

Put the pork shoulder in to cook after breakfast. The Brussels sprouts can be made ahead and reheated before serving, or cooked to be ready as supper is served. The cheesecake is a dose of sheer decadence and should be made in the morning as it needs to chill 8 hours before serving.

5-Ingredient Slow-Cooker
PULLED PORK

Serves 10   Hands-on 10 minutes   Total 8 hours, 10 minutes

2 large sweet onions, cut into ½-inch slices
1 (5- to 6-pound) boneless pork shoulder roast
  (Boston butt)
2 tablespoons garlic-oregano-red pepper
  seasoning blend
1 teaspoon kosher salt
1 (10½-ounce) can condensed chicken broth

1. Place onions in a lightly greased 6-quart slow cooker. Rub roast with seasoning blend and salt; place roast on onions. Pour broth over roast. Cover and cook on LOW 8 to 10 hours or until meat shreds easily with a fork.

2. Transfer roast to a cutting board or serving platter; shred with 2 forks, removing any large pieces of fat. Remove onions with a slotted spoon, and serve with pork.

BRUSSELS SPROUTS

with Pancetta

Serves 8   Hands-on 27 minutes   Total 27 minutes

2 pounds fresh Brussels sprouts, trimmed and halved
2 tablespoons olive oil
¼ teaspoon salt
¼ teaspoon freshly ground black pepper
6 (⅛-inch-thick) pancetta slices
1 tablespoon freshly grated Parmesan cheese

1. Preheat oven to 425°F. Toss together Brussels sprouts and next 3 ingredients in a 15- x 10-inch jelly-roll pan. Bake 17 to 20 minutes or until sprouts are tender and edges are lightly browned, stirring occasionally.

2. Meanwhile, cook pancetta in a large skillet over medium heat 8 to 10 minutes or until crisp. Remove pancetta, and drain on paper towels. Crumble pancetta.

3. Remove sprouts from oven, and place in a large serving dish. Top with cheese and crumbled pancetta.

Banana Pudding
CHEESECAKE

Serves 10 to 12 *Hands-on 45 minutes*
Total 11 hours, 10 minutes

1 ½ cups finely crushed vanilla wafers
½ cup chopped pecans
¼ cup butter, melted
17 vanilla wafers
2 large ripe bananas, diced
1 tablespoon lemon juice
2 tablespoons light brown sugar
3 (8-ounce) packages cream cheese, softened
1 cup granulated sugar
3 large eggs
2 teaspoons vanilla extract
½ cup coarsely crushed vanilla wafers
Garnishes: sweetened whipped cream, vanilla wafers,
   sliced bananas tossed in lemon juice

1. Preheat oven to 350°F. Stir together the first 3 ingredients in a small bowl until well blended. Press mixture onto bottom of a greased and floured 9-inch springform pan. Stand 17 vanilla wafers around the edge of the pan (rounded sides against pan), pressing gently into the crust to secure. Bake at 350°F for 10 minutes. Cool completely on a wire rack (about 30 minutes).

2. Combine bananas and lemon juice in a small saucepan. Stir in brown sugar. Cook over medium-high, stirring constantly, 1 minute or just until sugar has dissolved.

3. Beat cream cheese at medium speed with an electric mixer 3 minutes or until smooth. Gradually add granulated sugar, beating until blended. Add eggs, 1 at a time, beating just until yellow disappears after each addition. Beat in vanilla. Gently stir banana mixture into cream cheese mixture. Pour batter into prepared crust.

4. Bake at 350°F for 45 to 55 minutes or until center is almost set. Remove cheesecake from oven; gently run a knife around the edge of the cheesecake to loosen. Sprinkle top of cheesecake with coarsely crushed wafers. Cool completely on a wire rack (about 1 hour). Cover and chill 8 hours. Garnish as desired.

MENU THIRTEEN

SERVES 8-10

A spiral-cut ham is a traditional centerpiece for a Sunday meal, often for a holiday. Discard the glazing packet that comes with the ham and prepare this outstanding Southern Cola-Dijon-Brown Sugar Glaze. Use our foolproof blanching method for the Asparagus and Spring Peas and your vegetables will look as good as they taste. The ham needs about three and a half hours total prep and cook time, so start it in the afternoon. The vegetables can be blanched in advance and refrigerated. Sauté those in butter as directed just before serving. The chowchow is best made in advance and allowed to cool for 30 minutes, or refrigerate until needed. The rolls (pillowy biscuits, really) are best just out of the oven.

GLAZED SPIRAL-CUT HOLIDAY HAM (page 185)

ASPARAGUS AND SPRING PEAS WITH RED PEPPER CHOWCHOW (page 186)

PILLOWY BISCUIT ROLLS (page 188)

SET THE
SCENE

Not every occasion requires a tablecloth, and if you have a beautiful wood table, show it off.

Here the wood and the glazed china are contrasts that "go." Mix up the place setting using different patterns for the courses. And unite them all with a glorious and generously sized napkin. Footed glasses are overflowing with short-stemmed blossoms from the garden.

Flower frogs are unique card holders—even antique ones are found at yard sales—and we are using them to hold a conversation starter at each place with a debatable topic. Make up your own or start with some of ours like:

· Chocolate or vanilla?
· Cookie dough or already baked?
· What would you do if you won the lottery?
· What do you wish you were really good at?
· What holiday would you invent?
· If you could win any award, what would it be?

This Holiday Ham is seen year-round, but it is certainly at its peak for Easter menus. I love this glaze, even if I was raised on ham studded with cloves and decorated with pineapple slices.

Glazed Spiral-Cut
HOLIDAY HAM

Serves 8 to 10   *Hands-on 10 minutes*   *Total 3 hours, 25 minutes, including glaze*

1 (8- to 9-pound) fully cooked, bone-in
   spiral-cut ham half
Cola-Dijon-Brown Sugar Glaze

Preheat oven to 350°F. Place ham half, cut side down, in a heavy-duty aluminum foil-lined jelly-roll pan; let stand at room temperature 30 minutes. Brush ½ cup glaze over ham. Bake, uncovered, on lowest oven rack 2½ to 3 hours or until a meat thermometer inserted into thickest portion registers 140°F, basting every 30 minutes with ½ cup glaze. Remove from oven, and spoon pan drippings over ham. Let stand 10 minutes.

Cola-Dijon-Brown Sugar Glaze

Makes 1½ cups   *Hands-on 5 minutes*   *Total 5 minutes*

1½ cups firmly packed dark brown sugar
½ cup cola soft drink
½ cup Dijon mustard
½ teaspoon kosher salt

Stir together all ingredients until smooth.

If there are leftovers of ham, be ready to use them up in Hawaiian soft rolls slathered with spicy mustard or the honey variety. Slice ham into thin strips to top salads. Or, if you have 2 cups of diced or chopped ham, use it in the Maple Ham and French Toast Casserole on page 273.

ASPARAGUS AND SPRING PEAS
with Red Pepper Chowchow

Serves 8 to 10   Hands-on 25 minutes   Total 1 hour, 10 minutes, including chowchow

2 pounds fresh asparagus
Kosher salt
2 (8-ounce) packages fresh sugar snap peas, trimmed
2 (6-ounce) packages fresh English peas
1 tablespoon butter or olive oil
4 tablespoons Red Pepper Chowchow

1. Snap off and discard tough ends of asparagus. Bring a large pot of water to a boil. Stir in kosher salt until the water tastes as salty as the sea (about 1½ tablespoons per every 5 quarts of water). While the water returns to a boil, fill a large bowl halfway with ice cubes. Add just enough cold water to make the ice float.

2. Boil asparagus until it is bright green and crisp-tender (1 to 2 minutes). Transfer to a colander set in the ice water to set the color and texture, using a slotted spoon or tongs. Chill until ice-cold, then drain. Repeat procedure with sugar snap peas and English peas.

3. Melt butter in a large skillet over medium-high heat. Add asparagus, sugar snap peas, and English peas, and sauté 3 minutes or until thoroughly heated. Stir in Red Pepper Chowchow, and sauté 1 minute. Serve immediately.

Red Pepper Chowchow

Makes 1½ cups   Hands-on 15 minutes   Total 45 minutes

3 red bell peppers, chopped
½ medium-size sweet onion, chopped
3 garlic cloves, finely chopped
⅓ cup olive oil
¼ cup white wine vinegar
1¼ teaspoons kosher salt
½ teaspoon dried crushed red pepper
½ teaspoon orange zest

Sauté first 3 ingredients in hot oil in a large skillet 6 to 7 minutes or until tender. Add vinegar and next 3 ingredients to skillet, and sauté 2 minutes. Cool completely. Serve immediately, or refrigerate up to 1 week.

Pillowy
BISCUIT ROLLS

Makes 12 to 14 rolls   *Hands-on 25 minutes*
Total 50 minutes

½ cup shortening, frozen
2½ cups self-rising flour
1 cup chilled buttermilk
Parchment paper
2 tablespoons butter, melted

1. Preheat oven to 475°F. Grate frozen shortening using large holes of a box grater. Toss together grated shortening and flour in a medium bowl. Chill 10 minutes.

2. Make a well in center of mixture. Add buttermilk, and stir 15 times. Dough will be sticky.

3. Turn dough out onto a lightly floured surface. Lightly sprinkle flour over top of dough. Using a lightly floured rolling pin, roll dough into a ¾-inch-thick rectangle (about 9 x 5 inches). Fold dough in half so short ends meet. Repeat rolling and folding process 4 more times.

4. Roll dough to ½-inch thickness. Cut with a 2½-inch floured round cutter, reshaping scraps and flouring as needed.

5. Place dough rounds on a parchment paper–lined jelly-roll pan. Bake at 475°F for 15 minutes or until lightly browned. Brush with melted butter.

SOUTHERN SAVVY
HOME FOR THE HOLIDAY

Tensions can rise during mealtime when gathering disparate family members in one location. A good host can tame a bit of it by following a few simple guidelines. First, serve the meal on time—the longer guests wait for food, the more likely they are to over-imbibe at the bar. Next, make a seating chart to not only separate obvious foes, but also to encourage good conversation. And third, give troublemakers a job to do if the heat rises at the table—it will interrupt them from their argument and perhaps end it altogether.

SUNDAYS PAST & PRESENT
with PATRICK EVANS-HYLTON

Meet Patrick Evans-Hylton, a Johnson & Wales-trained chef and award-winning food writer, cookbook author, food educator, food historian, and overall culinary cheerleader.

HOMETOWN: Atlanta, GA **RESIDES:** Norfolk, VA

WHAT COMES TO MIND WHEN YOU THINK OF MEALS FROM SUNDAYS PAST?

I grew up in suburban Atlanta, raised by my paternal grandparents, and largely in the kitchen of my grandmother, Ma'am-Ma. It is there that I learned how to cook and learned to equate cooking with sharing and love. Ma'am-Ma cooked daily meals from scratch; hot biscuits and cornbread were always a part. But Sunday is when she really put on the dog. We'd get home from church, and supper was a big deal—a hot entrée and no fewer than a half-dozen sides, often including fried okra, sweet potato casserole, and pork-seasoned string beans, plus a glorious cake or pie. It was quite a spread, with trays of relishes and chowchows and a large pitcher of sweet ice tea.

WHAT DISH DID YOU LOOK FORWARD TO HAVING?

All of Ma'am-Ma's food was amazing, from fried chicken to pork chops, but her glazed ham was something special. It was usually reserved for Sundays, Easter, and Christmas. She'd rub it with seasoned brown sugar and drown it with chunked pineapple in its juice. The ham was further studded with cloves. I'd stand with her as she took it out of the oven a few times and basted it in those wonderful, fragrant bubbling juices covering it in foil the last little bit of cooking. I was usually rewarded with a taste before it made its way to the dining room table.

TELL US ABOUT YOUR FAVORITE SUNDAY SUPPER—PAST OR PRESENT.

One Easter, as a child, I remember coming back from the egg hunt at Stone Mountain Park with a basket full of spoils. The dinner was magical. The ham sat on a platter, an edible work of art, and the flavor was sublime. We lost Ma'am-Ma at age 87 at Christmas 2013, but so many Sundays my taste buds wander back to that sweet, salty, rich ham that almost looked too good to eat. Almost.

When a crowd gathers, a pot of simmering soup is sure to please.
Cornbread with Lemon-Thyme Butter accompanies this soup and is just right for a little dunking into the broth. The clever tiramisù is assembled in individual shot glasses. Feel free to assemble in a large glass bowl, lining the bowl with the ladyfingers. Select soft ladyfingers, found in the bakery or produce section of your supermarket.

Make the lemon curd ahead, and refrigerate up to a week. The tiramisù can be made early in the day and left to chill in the refrigerator, or at least given a two-hour chilling time. The cornbread assembles quickly, but plan time for it to cool before serving. The soup will need about two and a half hours. It can be made ahead, stopping before adding the spinach and remaining ingredients. Reheat when ready to serve, and complete the recipe.

Hearty Italian
SOUP

Makes 12 cups   *Hands-on 40 minutes*   *Total 1 hour, 5 minutes*

1 (16-ounce) package mild Italian sausage
2 teaspoons olive oil
1 large onion, diced
2 garlic cloves, minced
1 (48-ounce) container chicken broth
2 (15-ounce) cans cannellini beans, drained and rinsed
2 (14.5-ounce) cans diced tomatoes
1 teaspoon dried Italian seasoning
1 (5-ounce) package baby spinach
¼ cup chopped fresh parsley
¼ cup chopped fresh basil
Freshly shaved Parmesan cheese

Cook sausage in hot oil in a Dutch oven over medium heat 7 to 8 minutes on each side or until browned. Remove sausage from Dutch oven, reserving drippings in Dutch oven. Sauté onion in hot drippings 3 minutes or until tender. Add garlic, and sauté 1 minute. Cut sausage into ¼-inch-thick slices, and return to Dutch oven. Stir chicken broth and next 3 ingredients into sausage mixture; bring to a boil over medium-high heat. Reduce heat to medium-low, and simmer 25 minutes. Stir in spinach and next 2 ingredients; cook, stirring occasionally, 5 to 6 minutes or until spinach is wilted. Top each serving with Parmesan cheese.

CORNBREAD
with Lemon–Thyme Butter

Serves 8   *Hands-on 15 minutes*   *Total 1 hour*

3 tablespoons canola oil
1 cup stone-ground cornmeal
1 cup all-purpose flour
2 tablespoons granulated sugar
2 tablespoons baking powder
1 teaspoon kosher salt
2 large eggs
1¼ cups whole milk
2 tablespoons unsalted butter, melted
Lemon-Thyme Butter

1. Preheat oven to 425°F. Grease a 10-inch cast-iron skillet with oil. Place skillet in preheated oven until hot, about 5 minutes.

2. Combine cornmeal, flour, sugar, baking powder, and salt in a large bowl. Whisk together eggs, milk, and butter in a separate bowl, and add to cornmeal mixture, stirring just until combined. Carefully pour batter into hot skillet.

3. Bake at 425°F until golden brown, 15 to 20 minutes. Cool to room temperature in skillet, about 30 minutes. Serve with Lemon-Thyme Butter.

Lemon–Thyme Butter

Makes about 1 cup   *Hands-on 5 minutes*   *Total 5 minutes*

1 cup unsalted butter
1½ teaspoons lemon zest
1 tablespoon fresh lemon juice
1 teaspoon fresh thyme leaves
1 teaspoon kosher salt

Stir together all ingredients in a small bowl.

Lemon
TIRAMISÙ

Makes 24 shooters   Hands-on 30 minutes
Total 6 hours, 45 minutes, including lemon curd

1 (8-ounce) container mascarpone cheese
½ cup sugar
2 teaspoons vanilla extract
1 cup whipping cream
2 (3-ounce) packages ladyfingers
24 (1½-ounce) shot glasses
1½ cups Quick and Easy Lemon Curd
24 fresh raspberries
24 small fresh mint sprigs

1. Stir together first 3 ingredients just until blended.

2. Beat whipping cream at medium speed with an electric mixer until soft peaks form; fold into cheese mixture. Spoon mixture into a zip-top plastic freezer bag. (Do not seal.) Snip 1 corner of bag to make a ½-inch hole.

3. Cut ladyfingers in half crosswise. Press 1 ladyfinger half into bottom of each shot glass. Spoon 1½ teaspoons lemon curd into each glass. Pipe a small amount of mascarpone mixture into each glass. Repeat layers once with remaining ladyfingers, lemon curd, and mascarpone mixture. Top each with 1 raspberry and 1 mint sprig. Cover and chill 2 hours.

The lemon curd stores in an airtight container in the refrigerator up to 2 weeks. Spread it on English muffins or toast for a breakfast treat or fold it into whipped cream to fill a tart.

Quick and Easy Lemon Curd

Grate zest from 6 lemons to equal 2 tablespoons. Cut lemons in half; squeeze juice into a measuring cup to equal 1 cup. Beat ½ cup softened butter and 2 cups sugar at medium speed with an electric mixer until blended. Add 4 eggs, 1 at a time, beating just until blended after each addition. Gradually add lemon juice to butter mixture, beating at low speed just until blended after each addition; stir in zest. (Mixture will look curdled.) Transfer to a 3-quart microwave-safe bowl. Microwave at HIGH 5 minutes, stirring at 1-minute intervals. Microwave, stirring at 30-second intervals, 1 to 2 more minutes or until mixture thickens, coats the back of a spoon, and starts to mound slightly when stirred. Place heavy-duty plastic wrap directly on warm curd (to prevent a film from forming), and chill 4 hours or until firm. Makes 2 cups

Casseroles can be the easiest dish to serve a crowd, and this Baked Ziti with Sausage is mouthwateringly good. Ziti, Italian sausage, red wine, tomatoes, basil, ricotta, mozzarella—I could go on. The recipe also calls for pancetta, or cured pork belly, which is the same thing as bacon without the smoke (but feel free to substitute bacon). Find it in the deli case of most supermarkets. Native to Italy, San Marzano canned tomatoes are known for their sweet flavor. Consider trying them in place of regular crushed tomatoes in the sauce. The snap pea salad adds color and texture to the menu and is a great balance for the heavier main dish. Since our salad is so virtuous, let's have rich chocolate brownies for dessert.

Prepare the brownies earlier in the day, as they can sit at room temperature. The salad can be assembled any time, kept refrigerated, and dressed just before serving. The casserole can be made ahead and refrigerated prior to baking. If cold, place into a cold oven, then set the temperature. Add another 5 to 10 minutes to the baking time.

BAKED ZITI
with Sausage

Serves 8   *Hands-on 30 minutes*   *Total 55 minutes*

12 ounces uncooked ziti pasta
4 ounces pancetta or bacon, diced
1 large onion, chopped
3 garlic cloves, chopped
1 (1-pound) package ground Italian sausage
1 cup dry red wine
1 (28-ounce) can crushed tomatoes
½ cup firmly packed torn fresh basil
½ teaspoon kosher salt
½ teaspoon dried crushed red pepper
1 cup ricotta cheese
1 (8-ounce) package shredded mozzarella cheese
Vegetable cooking spray
½ cup grated Parmesan cheese

1. Preheat oven to 350°F. Prepare ziti according to package directions for al dente.

2. Meanwhile, cook pancetta in a large skillet over medium-high heat 3 minutes. Add onion and garlic, and sauté 3 minutes or until onion is tender. Add sausage, and sauté 5 minutes or until meat is no longer pink. Add wine, and cook 3 minutes. Stir in tomatoes and next 3 ingredients. Reduce heat to low, and cook, stirring occasionally, 3 minutes.

3. Stir ricotta and 1 cup mozzarella cheese into hot cooked pasta. Lightly grease a 13- x 9-inch baking dish with cooking spray. Transfer pasta mixture to prepared dish, and top with sausage mixture. Sprinkle with Parmesan cheese and remaining 1 cup mozzarella cheese.

4. Bake at 350°F for 25 to 30 minutes or until bubbly.

Sugar Snap
PEA SALAD

Serves 6 to 8 *Hands-on 15 minutes* *Total 15 minutes*

8 ounces sugar snap peas
2 cups mâche
2 cups chopped fresh cauliflower
½ cup chopped green onions
3 tablespoons chopped fresh dill weed
1 garlic clove, minced
1 tablespoon olive oil
1 tablespoon white wine vinegar
1 teaspoon salt

Cut sugar snap peas into 1-inch pieces. Cook in boiling water to cover 15 seconds; plunge in ice water. Drain. Toss together peas, mâche, cauliflower, green onions, dill weed, minced garlic, olive oil, vinegar, and salt.

Simple
BROWNIES
with Chocolate Frosting

Makes 4 dozen *Hands-on 15 minutes*
Total 1 hour, 56 minutes, including frosting

1 ½ cups coarsely chopped pecans
1 (4-ounce) unsweetened chocolate baking bar, chopped
¾ cup butter
2 cups sugar
4 large eggs
1 cup all-purpose flour
Chocolate Frosting

1. Preheat oven to 350°F. Bake pecans in a single layer in a shallow pan 6 to 8 minutes or until lightly toasted and fragrant.

2. Microwave chocolate and butter in a large microwave-safe bowl at HIGH 1 to 1 ½ minutes or until melted and smooth, stirring at 30-second intervals. Whisk in sugar and eggs until well blended. Stir in flour. Spread batter into a greased 13- x 9-inch pan.

3. Bake at 350°F for 25 to 30 minutes or until a wooden pick inserted in center comes out with a few moist crumbs.

4. Prepare Chocolate Frosting. Pour over warm brownies; spread to edges. Sprinkle with pecans. Let cool 1 hour on a wire rack. Cut into squares.

Chocolate Frosting

Makes 2 cups *Hands-on 10 minutes* *Total 10 minutes*

½ cup butter
⅓ cup milk
6 tablespoons unsweetened cocoa
1 (16-ounce) package powdered sugar
1 teaspoon vanilla extract

Cook first 3 ingredients over medium heat in a large saucepan, stirring constantly, 4 to 5 minutes or until butter melts. Remove from heat, and beat in powdered sugar and vanilla at medium speed with an electric mixer until smooth.

Chapter 4
LIGHTER SUPPERS

Traditionally in Southern cooking, Sunday supper was a light meal enjoyed in the evening, usually having had a big Sunday dinner at midday or early afternoon. Here you'll find some of our favorite lighter suppers, including sandwiches, soups, and salads. There is even a start to a tailgate menu or a cocktail party.

A cup of soup and a hot sandwich have always been a favorite supper for me, one I still enjoy today. It's a meal well suited to end a day that included a fancy restaurant brunch or a classic Sunday dinner. And almost always, fingers are involved—with sandwiches or little pick-up bites.

There's so much to enjoy here—*Smoky Chicken Panini, Mini Meatball Minestrone, Mini Muffulettas, Pulled Pork Tacos, Spicy Coconut Shrimp Soup,* and more—for eating in or toting elsewhere.

There are side dishes to mix and match, from *Watermelon "Steak" Salad* to *Avocado Fruit Salad* to *Tabbouleh Salad.* And we wouldn't forget dessert: How about *Peanut Butter-Banana Cream Pie* or *Key Lime Pie Ice Cream?* These are only the beginning.

MENU ONE
SERVES 4

SMOKY CHICKEN PANINI WITH BASIL MAYO (PAGE 201)

TABBOULEH SALAD (PAGE 202)

MIXED BERRIES WITH ORANGE MASCARPONE CREAM (PAGE 203)

Hot sandwiches make for a fine supper any night of the week. For this Sunday supper, we pair chicken breasts with a basil mayonnaise and smoked Gouda cheese. Since the sandwiches are prepared individually, it's easy to substitute everyone's favorite cheese. No panini press? No problem: Preheat a cast-iron skillet to medium-low. Add the sandwich, then press a heavy pan or clean brick wrapped in aluminum foil on top to weigh it down. Cook until golden and crisp, two to three minutes on each side. Cook the sandwiches over medium-low heat rather than high heat so the bread doesn't burn before the cheese melts. The refreshing scent of mint plays an important role in many Southern recipes, from iced tea to juleps. It's a key ingredient in this tabbouleh, which can also be served with simple grilled chicken, fish, or lamb.

Prepare the Tabbouleh Salad ahead—up to a day ahead—and chill. The mascarpone cream can also be made ahead and kept refrigerated. Wash the berries when ready to use them; dry them gently on paper towel-lined jelly-roll pans. Give them a gentle shake to remove excess water. Prepare sandwiches just before serving.

Smoky CHICKEN PANINI with Basil Mayo

Serves 4   Hands-on 35 minutes   Total 35 minutes

½ cup mayonnaise
2 tablespoons chopped fresh basil
½ teaspoon lemon zest
8 sourdough bread slices
4 cooked boneless chicken breasts (about 1 pound), sliced
½ pound smoked Gouda cheese, sliced
1 cup loosely packed baby spinach
¼ cup thinly sliced sun-dried tomatoes
3 tablespoons butter, melted

1. Stir together mayonnaise and next 2 ingredients. Spread mixture on 1 side of each bread slice. Top 4 bread slices with chicken, Gouda, and next 2 ingredients. Top with remaining bread slices, mayonnaise mixture sides down. Brush sandwiches with melted butter.

2. Cook sandwiches, in batches, in a preheated panini press 2 to 3 minutes or until golden brown.

Tabbouleh
SALAD

Serves 5   *Hands-on 20 minutes*   *Total 1 hour, 50 minutes*

1 cup uncooked bulgur wheat*
1 cup boiling water*
2 medium tomatoes, chopped
4 green onions, thinly sliced
¼ cup minced fresh parsley
¼ to ½ cup chopped fresh mint
½ teaspoon lemon zest
⅓ cup fresh lemon juice
3 tablespoons olive oil
½ teaspoon salt
½ teaspoon freshly ground black pepper
20 romaine lettuce leaves

1. Place bulgur in a large bowl, and add 1 cup boiling water. Cover and let stand 30 minutes.

2. Stir in tomato and next 8 ingredients. Chill 1 hour. Spoon into lettuce leaves just before serving.

*1 cup instant brown rice, cooked, may be substituted for 1 cup bulgur wheat and 1 cup boiling water.

MIXED BERRIES

with Orange Mascarpone Cream

Serves 6   *Hands-on 20 minutes*   *Total 20 minutes*

¼ cup mascarpone cheese
¼ cup vanilla
2% reduced-fat Greek yogurt
½ teaspoon grated orange rind
2 cups quartered strawberries
1 cup blueberries
1 cup raspberries
1 cup blackberries
1 tablespoon sugar
1 tablespoon chopped fresh mint
1 tablespoon fresh orange juice
Peeled orange curls (optional)
Mint leaves (optional)

1. Combine first 4 ingredients in a small bowl.

2. Combine strawberries and next 3 ingredients in a medium bowl. Gently stir in sugar, chopped mint, and orange juice. Spoon fruit mixture into bowls; top evenly with mascarpone cream. Garnish with orange curls and mint leaves, if desired.

This minestrone is a colorful crowd-pleaser, and it's only one hour from start to finish. If your family has never tried parsnips, this is the recipe to introduce them. The parsnips as they are chopped into bite-size pieces and mixed with other ingredients. The watermelon salad is not your mother's fruit salad. A cold, thick, steak-like slice of ripe watermelon pairs unexpectedly well with salty Cotija cheese and a smoky vinaigrette. Plan ahead to prepare the foolproof Peanut Butter-Banana Cream Pie so the crust and custard can meld in the refrigerator for 4 to 48 hours before topping with cream. The minestrone can be made up to a day ahead and reheated. Assemble salad just before serving.

Mini Meatball
MINESTRONE

Serves 8   *Hands-on 25 minutes*   *Total 47 minutes*

SOUP
1 tablespoon olive oil
2 cups diced onion
¾ cup (½-inch) sliced carrot
¾ cup (½-inch) sliced celery
¾ cup (½-inch) cubed parsnip
2 garlic cloves, minced
3 cups chopped Swiss chard
1 cup dry red wine
½ teaspoon freshly ground black pepper
¼ teaspoon kosher salt
1 (32-ounce) container beef broth
1 (14.5-ounce) can diced tomatoes with basil,
   garlic, and oregano

MINI MEATBALLS
1 pound ground turkey
3 tablespoons dry breadcrumbs
1 tablespoon chopped fresh basil
1 tablespoon olive oil
½ teaspoon freshly ground black pepper
¼ teaspoon kosher salt
1 large egg, lightly beaten

ADDITIONAL INGREDIENTS
1 (15-ounce) can chickpeas (garbanzo beans),
   rinsed and drained
¼ cup chopped fresh basil
1 ounce grated fresh Parmesan cheese (optional)

1. To prepare soup, heat a large Dutch oven over medium-high heat. Add oil; swirl to coat. Add onion and next 4 ingredients; sauté 6 minutes or until vegetables are tender. Add chard; sauté 1 minute or until wilted. Stir in wine and next 4 ingredients. Bring to a boil; reduce heat and simmer 10 minutes.

2. To prepare meatballs, combine turkey and next 6 ingredients in a bowl. Shape meat mixture by tablespoonfuls into 30 meatballs. Add meatballs and chickpeas to soup. Bring to a boil over medium-high heat. Cover and cook 12 minutes or until meatballs are done. Remove from heat; stir in ¼ cup basil.

3. Ladle soup into bowls, and sprinkle evenly with Parmesan cheese, if desired.

Watermelon "Steak" SALAD

Serves 8   Hands-on 30 minutes
Total 2 hours, 35 minutes, including dressing

1 medium-size red onion, sliced
1 cup seasoned rice wine vinegar
1 garlic clove, minced
1 tablespoon sugar
1½ teaspoons salt
12 cups assorted tender salad greens
   (such as mâche, watercress, arugula, and Bibb)
1 cup crumbled Cotija or feta cheese
Smoky Dijon Dressing
8 (1¼-inch-thick) chilled seedless watermelon slices, rinds removed
¾ cup salted pepitas or sunflower seeds

1. Stir together first 5 ingredients and ¼ cup water in a glass bowl. Cover and chill 2 hours. (Mixture can be made and chilled up to 2 days ahead.) Remove onions from marinade, discarding marinade.

2. Toss together greens, cheese, 1 cup red onions, and desired amount of dressing in a large bowl. Top each watermelon slice with 1½ cups greens mixture. Sprinkle with pepitas. Serve immediately with remaining dressing and onions.

Smoky Dijon Dressing

Makes about 1 cup   Hands-on 5 minutes   Total 5 minutes

⅔ cup olive oil
⅓ cup red wine vinegar
2 tablespoons honey
2 teaspoons pimentón (sweet smoked Spanish paprika)
2 teaspoons coarse-grained Dijon mustard
Kosher salt
Freshly ground black pepper

Whisk together olive oil, vinegar, honey, pimentón, and Dijon mustard. Add kosher salt and black pepper to taste.

Peanut Butter–Banana CREAM PIE

Serves 8   Hands-on 35 minutes   Total 5 hours, 45 minutes

22 peanut butter sandwich cookies
½ cup lightly salted dry-roasted peanuts
¼ cup butter, melted
½ cup granulated sugar
¼ cup cornstarch
2 cups half-and-half
4 large egg yolks
3 tablespoons butter
2 tablespoons creamy peanut butter
2 teaspoons vanilla extract
2 medium-size bananas
2 cups heavy cream
½ cup powdered sugar

1. Preheat oven to 350°F. Process cookies and peanuts in a food processor about 1 minute or until finely chopped. Stir together cookie mixture and melted butter. Press crumb mixture on bottom, up sides, and onto lip of a lightly greased 9-inch pie plate.

2. Bake at 350°F for 10 to 12 minutes or until lightly browned. Transfer to a wire rack, and cool completely (about 30 minutes).

3. Whisk together granulated sugar and cornstarch in a large, heavy saucepan. Whisk together half-and-half and egg yolks in a medium bowl. Gradually whisk half-and-half mixture into sugar mixture, and bring to a boil over medium heat, whisking constantly. Boil, whisking constantly, 1 minute; remove from heat.

4. Stir butter, peanut butter, and 1 teaspoon vanilla into sugar mixture. Place heavy-duty plastic wrap directly on warm custard (to prevent a film from forming), and cool 30 minutes.

5. Cut bananas into ½-inch-thick slices; place in a single layer on bottom of crust, covering bottom completely. Spoon custard mixture over bananas; cover and chill 4 to 48 hours.

6. Beat cream at high speed with an electric mixer until foamy; gradually add powdered sugar and remaining 1 teaspoon vanilla, beating until soft peaks form. Top pie with whipped cream mixture. Serve immediately, or chill up to 4 hours.

MENU THREE

SERVES 8

Muffulettas are the famous sandwich of New Orleans, filled with pickled vegetables, olives, meats, and cheeses. These are a miniature version, just right for eating out of hand. The Apple Coleslaw is tart, bright, and crisp. Try an apple you may not have used before, such as Pink Lady or Honeycrisp. In keeping with the New Orleans theme, Cajun Lemonade is an adults-only dose of refreshment using rum, hot sauce, and lemonade. Prepare the muffulettas early so they have a chance to chill. They can even be made a day ahead. The base for the lemonade may be made ahead, and the club soda added just before serving.

**MINI
MUFFULETTAS** (page 211)

**APPLE
COLESLAW** (page 212)

**CAJUN
LEMONADE** (page 214)

SET THE
SCENE

Cheer on your team with this game day menu perfect for the next tailgate or in front of the big screen at home.

Game day automatically gives you a color scheme for inspiration, and the possibilities are endless. We picked up some checkered paper wraps and flags to carry the theme through the food.

This menu can be multiplied for a crowd, and it's always easy to add tasty dips (store-bought or homemade) to serve with fresh celery, carrot, and pepper dippers. These muffulettas fit right in your hand and are protein-packed for sustenance.

Make your own snack mix by combining perennial favorites like mixed nuts, thin pretzels, bite-size bagel chips, and rice, corn, and wheat cereal squares. And who would really mind if you gild the lily by tossing in candy-coated chocolates?

To expand the menu, or provide finger food for the kids, pick up a tray of chicken fingers or make your own. Bamboo or toothpicks can hold team flags and make dipping easy.

Set up a blind tasting for beer using small disposable cups numbered with permanent marker, and have your guests each bring their favorite to share. It's especially fun to try local craft beers to see which ones are your favorites. Not a beer fan? Mix up a batch of adult lemonade, and ladle it from a large glass vessel to serve.

Mini
MUFFULETTAS

Serves 12   Hands-on 25 minutes   Total 25 minutes

2 (16-ounce) jars mixed pickled vegetables
¾ cup pimiento-stuffed Spanish olives, chopped
2 tablespoons bottled olive oil-and-vinegar dressing
12 small dinner rolls, cut in half
6 Swiss cheese slices, cut in half
12 thin deli ham slices
12 Genoa salami slices
6 provolone cheese slices, cut in half

1. Pulse pickled vegetables in food processor 8 to 10 times or until finely chopped. Stir in olives and dressing.

2. Spread 1 heaping tablespoonful pickled vegetable mixture over cut side of each roll bottom. Top each with 1 Swiss cheese slice half, 1 ham slice, 1 salami slice, 1 provolone cheese slice half, and roll tops. Cover with plastic wrap. Serve immediately, or chill until ready to serve.

Look for jarred Italian "giardiniera" for the pickled vegetables called for in this recipe. This marinated vegetable medley typically includes bell peppers, celery, carrots, cauliflower, onions, pickles, and pepperoncini. It's the ideal mix for this for this Italian-inspired sandwich with New Orleans' roots.

Apple
COLESLAW

Serves 8   *Hands-on 15 minutes*   *Total 15 minutes*

¼ cup apple cider vinegar
2 tablespoons Dijon mustard
2 tablespoons honey
¾ teaspoon salt
¼ teaspoon freshly ground black pepper
¼ cup canola oil
2 (10-ounce) packages shredded coleslaw mix
4 green onions, sliced
2 celery ribs, sliced
2 small Honeycrisp, Gala, or Pink Lady apples, chopped

Whisk together first 5 ingredients. Gradually add oil in a slow, steady stream, whisking constantly until blended. Stir together coleslaw mix and next 3 ingredients in a large bowl; add vinegar mixture, tossing to coat.

VARIATIONS

Pear *Coleslaw:* Prepare recipe as directed, substituting Bosc pears for apples.

Cranberry-Almond *Coleslaw:* Omit apples. Prepare recipe as directed, stirring in 1 cup chopped, smoked almonds and ¾ cup sweetened dried cranberries.

Cajun
LEMONADE

Serves 8   Hands-on 5 minutes   Total 5 minutes

2 cups light rum
1 (12-ounce) can frozen lemonade concentrate, thawed
1 teaspoon hot sauce
1 (1-liter) bottle club soda, chilled
Crushed ice

Stir together first 3 ingredients. Add club soda just before serving. Serve over crushed ice.

SOUTHERN SAVVY
THE MORNING AFTER

Most guests are well intentioned and do think to thank their host. Some even break out the stationery and send a proper thank you in the mail. No matter your choice, it should be done the very next day. A simple phone call to share your appreciation of the event is the very least that should be done. A handwritten note mailed right away is even better, especially to share close sentiment. For a host who has thrown a party for you, a generous gift, either mailed or delivered in person, is essential.

SUNDAYS PAST & PRESENT
with JENNIFER CHANDLER

Meet Jennifer Chandler, cookbook author and restaurant consultant whose most recent book is *The Southern Pantry Cookbook: 105 Recipes Already Hiding in Your Kitchen.*

HOMETOWN: Memphis, TN RESIDES: Memphis, TN

WHAT COMES TO MIND WHEN YOU THINK OF MEALS FROM SUNDAYS PAST?

Sunday supper is a tradition in our family. It is the day that we slow down our busy pace of life. The whole family (and often some friends that might just as well be kin) gather around the table for a lazy and delicious meal. So much of Southern living is spent in the kitchen and around the dinner table. My most cherished memories of my family are centered around a meal. My dad's family is from New Orleans, and, in my honest opinion, his mom was the best cook in the world. This demure French Creole woman could cook up a storm. I don't think I ever had a meal from her kitchen that was not delicious. I have vivid memories of standing on my tiptoes to peer into the pots simmering on her stovetop, helping her slice the French bread, and giggling with my cousins at the kids' table. Whether I host or my Dad does, I have continued the tradition of Sunday suppers for my family in hopes that my children will have the same fond memories of their family and childhood that I do.

WHAT DISH DID YOU LOOK FORWARD TO HAVING?

Grillades over grits has been a family favorite as long as I can remember. When I was a little girl, my grandmother would make it for our Sunday get-togethers. The whole extended family (often 20-plus of us) would gather at her house for a delicious dinner featuring this Louisiana specialty. It's a dish that she served with love at family gatherings, and following in her footsteps, I do for my family now.

TELL US ABOUT YOUR FAVORITE SUNDAY SUPPER—PAST OR PRESENT.

My favorite Sunday suppers are the ones where the whole family is in the kitchen together helping put together the meal. These days, most of our Sunday suppers are actually a midday meal after church. We all come home, throw on aprons, and start cooking. The kids help with the prep and set the table. My husband opens a bottle of wine. Standing around the kitchen island, we giggle, tell stories, and catch up. Sometimes the meal is fancy; most often not. But there is always good food made with love together as a family. And we know the day is perfect if someone is found napping on the couch after all the dishes have been cleaned and put away.

MENU FOUR

SERVES 4-6

**SPICY COCONUT
SHRIMP SOUP** (PAGE 217)

**AVOCADO
FRUIT SALAD** (PAGE 218)

**KEY LIME PIE
ICE CREAM** (PAGE 219)

Tropical flavors abound in this Sunday supper menu that's a snap to prepare. Don't fear the long ingredients list for the Spicy Coconut Shrimp Soup—each ingredient contributes to the rich, complex flavor of the soup, and they all come together quickly in the pot. The Avocado Fruit Salad cools the palate, making it a superb pairing with the soup. Key Lime Pie Ice Cream is the ultimate end to this menu.

Prepare the ice cream up to a day ahead. The salad needs to chill at least an hour before serving. Prep all the ingredients for the soup in advance, as they are added to the pot in quick succession.

Spicy
COCONUT SHRIMP SOUP

Serves 4 to 6 *Hands-on 55 minutes* *Total 55 minutes*

1 pound unpeeled, medium-size raw
  Gulf shrimp
1 tablespoon grated fresh ginger
4 garlic cloves, minced
2 teaspoons olive oil
4 cups vegetable broth
1 (13.5-ounce) can unsweetened coconut milk
2½ tablespoons fish sauce
1 tablespoon light brown sugar
1 tablespoon fresh lime juice
2 teaspoons red curry paste
1 (8-ounce) package sliced fresh mushrooms
1 medium-size red bell pepper, chopped
¼ cup chopped fresh basil
¼ cup chopped fresh cilantro
¼ cup sliced green onions
1 Thai chile pepper, seeded and minced (optional)

1. Peel shrimp; devein, if desired.

2. Sauté ginger and garlic in hot oil in a large Dutch oven over medium-high heat 1 to 2 minutes or until fragrant. Add broth and next 5 ingredients. Bring broth mixture to a boil, and reduce heat to medium. Add mushrooms and bell pepper, and cook, stirring often, 3 to 5 minutes or until crisp-tender. Add shrimp, and cook 1 to 2 minutes or just until shrimp turn pink. Remove from heat. Add basil, next 2 ingredients, and, if desired, chile pepper.

Avocado
FRUIT SALAD

Makes 6 cups   Hands-on 15 minutes
Total 1 hour, 15 minutes

1 (24-ounce) jar refrigerated orange and grapefruit sections, drained,
   rinsed, and patted dry
1 (24-ounce) jar refrigerated tropical mixed fruit in light syrup, drained,
   rinsed, and patted dry
2 cups cubed fresh cantaloupe
1 medium-size ripe avocado, halved and cut into chunks
¼ cup chopped fresh mint
2 tablespoons lime juice

Toss together all ingredients. Cover and chill 1 hour.

Key Lime Pie
ICE CREAM

Makes about 1 quart *Hands-on 20 minutes*
Total 9 hours, 20 minutes

½ cup granulated sugar
2 tablespoons cornstarch
⅛ teaspoon salt
2 cups 2% reduced-fat milk
1 cup half-and-half
1 egg yolk
1 teaspoon Key lime zest
⅓ cup Key lime juice
½ cup coarsely crushed graham crackers

1. Whisk together first 3 ingredients in a large heavy saucepan. Gradually whisk in milk and half-and-half. Cook over medium heat, stirring constantly, 8 to 10 minutes or until mixture thickens slightly. Remove from heat.

2. Whisk egg yolk until slightly thickened. Gradually whisk about 1 cup hot cream mixture into yolk. Add yolk mixture to remaining cream mixture, whisking constantly.

3. Pour mixture through a fine wire-mesh strainer into a bowl, discarding solids. Cool 1 hour, stirring occasionally. Place plastic wrap directly on cream mixture; chill 8 to 24 hours.

4. Pour mixture into freezer container of a 1½-quart electric ice-cream maker, and freeze according to manufacturer's instructions; stir in Key lime zest, Key lime juice, and crushed graham crackers halfway through freezing. Let stand at room temperature 5 to 10 minutes before serving.

This is a light, simple seafood supper. The tilapia is coated with finely chopped almonds and is pan-sautéed in a mixture of butter and oil for maximum flavor and crunch. The Tomato-Cucumber Salad represents the best of summer in the South using vine-ripened tomatoes and the ubiquitous summertime cooler, the cucumber. The tropical Mango-Lime Sorbet is the perfect finish to this supper.

Prepare the sorbet up to a day ahead. The salad arrives on the table in 10 minutes or less, but prepare it before cooking the fish. It can sit at room temperature until the fish is ready. Use a skillet large enough to hold all the fillets comfortably, or cook them in batches. Substitute catfish, flounder, or orange roughy for tilapia, if desired.

Almond-Crusted
TILAPIA

Serves 4   Hands-on 20 minutes   Total 20 minutes

1 cup sliced almonds
¼ cup all-purpose flour
4 (6-ounce) tilapia fillets
½ teaspoon salt
2 tablespoons butter
2 tablespoons olive oil

1. Process ½ cup almonds in a food processor until finely chopped, and combine with flour in a shallow bowl.

2. Sprinkle fish evenly with salt; dredge in almond mixture.

3. Melt butter with olive oil in a large heavy skillet over medium heat; add fish, and cook 4 minutes on each side or until golden. Remove fillets to a serving plate.

4. Add remaining ½ cup almonds to skillet, and cook, stirring often, 1 minute or until golden. Remove almonds with a slotted spoon, and sprinkle over fish.

Tomato – Cucumber
SALAD

Serves 4 *Hands-on 10 minutes* *Total 10 minutes*

1 seedless cucumber, sliced
½ small onion, thinly sliced
2 cups quartered small, vine-ripened tomatoes
¼ cup olive oil-and-vinegar dressing
½ teaspoon lemon zest
1 tablespoon lemon juice

Stir together cucumber, onion, and tomatoes. Add dressing, lemon zest, lemon juice, and salt and pepper to taste. Toss to coat.

Mango–Lime
SORBET

Serves 8   *Hands-on 6 minutes*   *Total 2 hours, 6 minutes*

2 ¼ cups mango puree (4 mangoes)
½ cup plain Simple Syrup
1 teaspoon grated lime rind
2 teaspoons fresh lime juice
Lime zest (optional)

1. Combine first 4 ingredients in a bowl. Cover and chill 1 hour.

2. Pour mixture into the freezer can of an ice-cream freezer; freeze according to manufacturer's instructions. Spoon sorbet into a freezer-safe container; cover and freeze 1 hour or until firm. Garnish with lime zest, if desired.

Simple Syrup

Bring 1 cup water and 1 cup sugar to a boil in a small saucepan, stirring until sugar dissolves; boil 1 minute. Remove from heat, and let cool 30 minutes. Makes 2 cups

Taco night! Slow-cooked pork shoulder is the easiest dish ever and just right for nestling into a tortilla. The Avocado-Peach Salsa is a Southern take on a Southwest staple. Golden corn cut fresh off the cob is bursting with flavor. Enjoy this recipe year-round by substituting frozen corn. Choose your favorite berries to star in tasty little cobblers, served in individual-size skillets. Set the pork to begin cooking early in the day—at least eight hours before serving. Make the salsa to allow for at least one hour of chilling time.

PULLED PORK TACOS
with Avocado-Peach Salsa

Serves 10   Hands-on 27 minutes   Total 8 hours, 42 minutes, including salsa

2 tablespoons ground cumin
2 tablespoons ground coriander
2 teaspoons garlic powder
¾ teaspoon salt
½ teaspoon freshly ground black pepper
¼ teaspoon ground red pepper
3 pounds boneless pork shoulder roast (Boston butt)
1 tablespoon vegetable oil
1 large sweet onion, vertically sliced
1 cup reduced-sodium fat-free chicken broth
¼ cup apple cider vinegar
3 tablespoons brown sugar
20 (6-inch) fajita-size 96% fat-free flour tortillas
Avocado-Peach Salsa

1. Combine first 6 ingredients; remove 1 tablespoon spice mixture for onions. Sprinkle remaining spice mixture over pork. Cook pork in hot oil in a large skillet over medium-high heat 2 to 3 minutes on all sides, or until browned. Remove pork from skillet; place in a 5-quart slow cooker. Add onions to skillet; sprinkle with reserved 1 tablespoon spice mixture, and sauté 5 minutes or until golden brown. Add chicken broth, vinegar, and brown sugar. Remove from heat; pour over pork in slow cooker.

2. Cover and cook on LOW 8 hours or until pork is fork-tender. Transfer pork to a cutting board, reserving 1 cup cooking liquid; let stand 10 minutes. Shred pork with 2 forks. Toss pork with reserved 1 cup cooking liquid.

3. Warm tortillas according to package directions. Serve pork with tortillas and Avocado-Peach Salsa.

Avocado-Peach *Salsa*

Toss together 2 peeled and diced peaches, 2 seeded and diced plum tomatoes, 1 diced avocado, ¼ cup peeled and diced jicama, 1 tablespoon minced red onion, 3 tablespoons lime juice, 1 teaspoon olive oil, ¼ teaspoon salt, and ¼ teaspoon ground red pepper in a large bowl. Cover and chill until ready to serve.

Corn and Black Bean
SALAD

Serves 8   *Hands-on 15 minutes*   *Total 37 minutes*

2 cups fresh corn kernels (about 3 ears)
1 (15-ounce) can black beans, drained and rinsed
1 cup chopped tomato
⅓ cup lime juice
⅓ cup finely chopped red onion
½ jalapeño pepper, seeded and chopped
2 tablespoons chopped fresh cilantro
2 teaspoons hot sauce
½ teaspoon salt
½ teaspoon ground cumin
½ teaspoon ground coriander
½ teaspoon freshly ground black pepper

1. Preheat broiler with oven rack 5 inches from heat. Place corn kernels on an aluminum foil–lined baking sheet.

2. Broil corn 12 minutes or until lightly browned, stirring once. Remove from oven, and let stand 10 minutes.

3. Combine corn and remaining ingredients in a large bowl. Cover and chill at least 1 hour, until ready to serve.

We've kept this pasta dish on the light side for our Sunday supper, but for a heartier meal, substitute an equal amount of sausage- or meat-filled ravioli for the cheese-filled. If you have extra tomatoes on hand, add those to the batch being broiled, then reserve some to add to omelets, salads, or sandwiches during the week. The Cucumber and Sugar Snap Salad is light, but full of flavor. Edamame beans and strips of radish pack a punch of protein and flavor. For dessert, pears sautéed in butter and brown sugar might steal the show.

Prepare the salad up to four hours in advance, but allow at least one hour for chilling. No cukes or sugar snaps on hand? Almost any raw veggie will do. Try using bell peppers, jicama, or fresh corn kernels. The tomatoes can be broiled and left to rest until needed, or prepared along with the pasta as directed. The pasta dish takes just 15 minutes, if the ingredients are prepped ahead. The brown sugar pears are a quick dessert—perhaps made while someone else does the dishes?

PASTA
with Burst Tomatoes and Mascarpone

Serves 6   Hands-on 15 minutes   Total 15 minutes

1 (24-ounce) package frozen cheese-filled ravioli
3 pints assorted grape tomatoes
1 large tomato, chopped
2 garlic cloves, chopped
2 tablespoons olive oil
¼ cup butter, cubed
1 tablespoon fresh lemon juice
¾ teaspoon kosher salt
¼ teaspoon freshly ground black pepper
½ cup torn assorted fresh herbs
   (such as parsley and basil)
1 (8-ounce) container mascarpone cheese

1. Prepare pasta according to package directions, and keep warm.

2. Meanwhile, preheat broiler with oven rack 4 to 5 inches from heat. Stir together tomatoes, garlic, and olive oil in a 15- x 10-inch jelly-roll pan. Broil 5 to 8 minutes or until tomatoes are charred, stirring halfway through.

3. Transfer tomato mixture to a large bowl. Stir in butter, next 3 ingredients, and ¼ cup fresh herbs. Spoon over hot cooked ravioli; dollop with cheese. Sprinkle with remaining ¼ cup fresh herbs. Serve immediately.

Cucumber and Sugar Snap SALAD

Serves 8   *Hands-on 20 minutes*   *Total 20 minutes*

¼ cup Greek yogurt
¼ cup sour cream
1 garlic clove, minced
2 tablespoons chopped fresh mint
1 tablespoon chopped fresh dill
½ teaspoon kosher salt
½ teaspoon freshly ground black pepper
1 ounce feta cheese, crumbled
1 cup fully cooked shelled frozen edamame (green soybeans), thawed
1 cup fresh sugar snap peas, cut into ¼-inch pieces
½ English cucumber, diced (about 1 cup)
2 celery ribs, diced (about 1 cup)
6 to 8 radishes, cut into thin strips (about ⅓ cup)
¼ cup finely chopped red onion

1. Stir together first 7 ingredients in a small bowl; stir in feta cheese.

2. Toss together edamame and next 5 ingredients in a large bowl. Stir yogurt mixture into vegetable mixture. Serve immediately, or cover and chill up to 4 hours.

Brown Sugar
PEARS

Serves 4 *Hands-on 15 minutes* *Total 15 minutes*

1 tabespoon lemon juice
3 Anjou pears, peeled and quartered
3 tablespoons butter
¼ cup firmly packed brown sugar
1 teaspoon vanilla extract
Crème fraîche or vanilla ice cream
Gingersnaps, crumbled

1. Sprinkle lemon juice over pears; toss.

2. Melt 1 tablespoon butter in a large nonstick skillet over medium-high heat. Sauté pears 2 minutes or until browned. Add remaining 2 tablespoons butter and brown sugar to skillet. Reduce heat to medium-low; cook, stirring often, 3 to 4 minutes or until pears are tender. Remove from heat, and stir in vanilla extract.

3. Serve warm pears and syrup with a dollop of crème fraîche or ice cream. Sprinkle with gingersnap crumbs.

MENU EIGHT

SERVES 8

Easy and light, this summer salad is all crunch and flavor. Haricots verts (thin green beans), yellow wax beans, and sugar snap peas are blanched briefly, then chilled with radishes, walnuts, and little green peas. A mustard, pecorino, and anchovy dressing brings it all together. Cocktails featuring the tastes of summer—Kirby cucumbers muddled in gin, and tomatoes with mint muddled in tequila—are sure to be a hit. This menu should be made early in the afternoon to allow for each dish to be well chilled before serving. The cukes and peppers can be made up to 24 hours in advance.

SNAPPY BEANS AND PEAS
WITH PECORINO (page 235)

CUCUMBER
GIN AND TONIC (page 236)

TOMATO-TEQUILA
FIZZ (page 236)

SWEET-HOT CUKES AND
PEPPERS (page 238)

SET THE
SCENE

Who doesn't love a cocktail party?

I have longed to re-create the cocktail parties of the 1950s where the women wore cocktail dresses and the men wore ties. The glassware is so charming from that era, and it's one of my favorite items to collect.

No matter the season and no matter the style, an invitation to a cocktail party is almost always replied to with a yes. Here we have the perfect menu for a no-cook summer party sure to please.

These recipes highlight the season's best. In fact, it's vegetarian. Fresh garden peas and beans are the star of this elegant summer salad topped with walnuts (or use pecans) and Parmesan cheese. The cucumber and pepper salad is really refreshing. These recipes multiply up easily if you plan to invite the neighborhood. Even the cocktails get in on the act with fresh cucumbers and fresh tomatoes and mint. Supplement these make-ahead dishes with a cheese plate filled with pimiento cheese and a round of brie and maybe a chunk of Parmigiano Reggiano. A bowl of olives, a bowl of nuts, and if they're in season, some sliced fresh figs complete the platter.

Expanding the menu is easy by making it a potluck where guests bring a cold salad to share. It lightens your load and increases the enjoyment.

Snappy
BEANS AND PEAS
with Pecorino

Serves 8   *Hands-on 30 minutes*   *Total 1 hour, 30 minutes*

1 cup grated pecorino or Parmesan cheese
   (about 1½ ounce)
½ cup olive oil
¼ cup fresh lemon juice
1 garlic clove, minced
1 teaspoon anchovy paste
1 teaspoon Dijon mustard
½ pound haricots verts (thin green beans),
   trimmed and cut into thirds
½ pound fresh yellow wax beans, trimmed
½ pound sugar snap peas, trimmed
2 cups thinly sliced radicchio
⅔ cup roasted walnut halves
½ cup frozen green peas, thawed
1 large shallot, finely chopped
¼ cup thinly sliced chives

1. Process cheese, olive oil, lemon juice, garlic, anchovy paste, and Dijon mustard in a blender until smooth; add salt and black pepper to taste.

2. Place haricots verts and 2 cups water in a microwave-safe bowl. Cover tightly with plastic wrap, folding back a small edge to allow steam to escape. Microwave at HIGH 2 to 3 minutes or until crisp-tender; plunge into ice water. Drain; pat dry. Repeat with yellow wax beans and sugar snap peas.

3. Combine beans, sugar snap peas, radicchio, walnut halves, green peas, shallot, and chives. Chill up to 1 hour. Add desired amount of olive oil mixture to bean mixture; toss to coat. Sprinkle with salt and pepper to taste before serving.

Cucumber
GIN AND TONIC

Makes 4 cups   *Hands-on 5 minutes*   *Total 1 hour, 5 minutes*

4 Kirby cucumbers
3 limes
2 cups gin
½ cup tonic concentrate (such as Jack Rudy Cocktail Co. Small Batch Tonic)
2 cups chilled club soda

1. Cut 3 Kirby cucumbers into ½-inch-thick slices and 2 limes into 6 wedges; muddle in a bowl to release flavors. Stir in gin and tonic concentrate; let stand 30 minutes. Press through a fine wire-mesh strainer into a large container, using back of a spoon. Discard solids.

2. Cover and chill 1 to 2 hours. Cut remaining 1 Kirby cucumber and remaining 1 lime into ¼-inch-thick slices. Fill a large pitcher with ice cubes; add cucumber and lime slices. Stir in gin mixture and chilled club soda.

Tomato – Tequila
FIZZ

Makes 6 cups   *Hands-on 5 minutes*   *Total 1 hour, 5 minutes*

¾ cup grape tomato halves
¼ cup loosely packed mint leaves
1 lime, cut into wedges
¼ teaspoon kosher salt
2 cups tequila
¼ cup light agave nectar
¼ cup grape tomato halves
Fresh mint sprigs
4 cups chilled club soda

1. Muddle ¾ cup grape tomato halves, ¼ cup loosely packed mint leaves, lime wedges, and kosher salt in a medium bowl to release flavors. Stir in tequila and light agave nectar; let stand 15 minutes. Press mixture through a fine wire-mesh strainer into a large container, using back of a spoon. Discard pulp and seeds.

2. Cover and chill 1 to 2 hours. Fill a large pitcher with ice cubes; add ¼ cup grape tomato halves and fresh mint sprigs. Add chilled tomato mixture and chilled club soda. Stir gently.

Sweet-Hot
CUKES AND PEPPERS

Serves 8   *Hands-on 30 minutes*   *Total 3 hours, 30 minutes*

1½ large English cucumbers, thinly sliced (about 1 pound)
1 (8-ounce) package sweet mini bell peppers, thinly sliced
½ medium-size red onion, sliced
1 or 2 serrano peppers, seeded and thinly sliced
2 garlic cloves, minced
2 teaspoons kosher salt
⅓ cup Champagne vinegar
¼ cup sugar
1 tablespoon toasted sesame seeds
½ teaspoon mustard seeds
¼ teaspoon celery seeds

Stir together cucumbers, bell peppers, onion, serrano peppers, garlic, and kosher salt in a large bowl. Stir together vinegar, sugar, sesame seeds, mustard seeds, and celery seeds in a small bowl. Let both mixtures stand, stirring occasionally, 1 hour. Drain cucumber mixture. (Do not rinse.) Pour vinegar mixture over cucumber mixture; stir to coat. Chill 2 to 24 hours. Serve with a slotted spoon.

SOUTHERN SAVVY
WALLFLOWER

Everyone gets a little bit conversation-shy at one time or another, and even experienced party-goers can get tongue-tied. If you find it hard to start conversation, remember that most people enjoy talking about themselves! It is so much easier to ask a question and let the responder take it from there. Be a good listener, though, and ask follow-up questions to show you've been paying attention. Don't know what to ask? Brush up on the headlines of the day—a good news story, sports team scores, or travel discussions are all good ice breakers.

SUNDAYS PAST & PRESENT
with REBECCA LANG

Meet Rebecca Lang, cookbook author, mother of two, ninth-generation Southerner.

HOMETOWN: McRae, GA **RESIDES:** Athens, GA

WHAT COMES TO MIND WHEN YOU THINK OF MEALS FROM SUNDAYS PAST?

Our day of rest was an evolving one starting at the table and ending on the sofa. Sunday lunches were centered around plates overflowing with the most comforting of Southern foods. Fried chicken, deviled eggs, casseroles, biscuits, and homemade pickles made a weekly appearance. By early afternoon, all of my family could be found sprawled out in my grandmother's living room napping after the decadent meal. It was the utmost of family time that centered each of us for the next six days.

WHAT DISH DID YOU LOOK FORWARD TO HAVING?

Each Saturday afternoon brought cravings of fried chicken hopefully to appear on Sunday's menu. The moment the storm door opened to my grandmother's house, I knew immediately if Sunday lunch was centered around the coveted gospel bird or pork chops or cubed steak. When her cast-iron skillet was filled with chicken, heavenly aromas of fried temptations would sneak out even before we could announce we were coming in.

TELL US ABOUT YOUR FAVORITE SUNDAY SUPPER—PAST OR PRESENT.

After such a large midday meal, Sunday suppers were casual and much lighter. My favorite was my dad's fried egg sandwiches. White bread, ketchup, and one egg, fried just right to create only a trickle of yolk on the third bite. The thoughtful pairing consisted of skim milk in a juice glass. It was the perfect ending to such a filling day. As long as I live, I suspect I will prefer egg sandwiches on Sunday nights.

MENU NINE

SERVES 8-10

TORTILLA SOUP (PAGE 241)

**PEPPER JELLY &
GOAT CHEESE CAKES** (PAGE 242)

**ESPRESSO SHORTBREAD
COOKIES** (PAGE 243)

Soup and the slow cooker are a natural combination, and this Tortilla Soup doesn't disappoint. Chicken thighs, corn, and tomatoes and green chiles combine with smoked paprika, cumin, and chili powder for a just-right mix of heat and flavor. In the South, pepper jelly is often served with cream cheese and crackers as a savory snack. This upscale version served atop goat cheese cakes adds toasted pecans and a touch of hot sauce. Grind pecans in a food processor for the best texture. Serve it as an appetizer while assembling the soup toppings. The espresso shortbread cookies are a favorite to accompany tea and coffee.

Start the soup early in the day to allow for the eight hours of cooking time. The appetizers can be made early as well, as they can chill up to 12 hours before serving. The cookies can be made a day or two ahead or in the afternoon.

TORTILLA SOUP

Makes 10 cups　　　*Hands-on 10 minutes*　　　*Total 7 hours, 10 minutes*

1 ¾ pounds skinned and boned chicken thighs
1 (12-ounce) bag frozen whole kernel yellow corn, thawed
1 large onion, chopped
2 garlic cloves, pressed
2 (14-ounce) cans chicken broth
1 (14-ounce) can tomato puree
1 (10-ounce) can diced tomatoes and green chiles
1 teaspoon smoked paprika
2 teaspoons ground cumin
1 teaspoon chili powder
1 bay leaf
4 (5½-inch) corn tortillas
Toppings: fresh cilantro, shredded Cheddar cheese, sliced jalapeños, avocados

1. Combine first 11 ingredients in a 4-quart slow cooker.

2. Cover and cook on HIGH 7 to 8 hours. Discard bay leaf, and shred chicken.

3. Preheat oven to 375°F. Cut tortillas into ¼-inch-wide strips, and place on a baking sheet.

4. Bake at 375°F for 5 minutes. Stir, and bake 5 more minutes or until crisp. Add table salt to taste. Serve soup with tortilla strips and desired toppings.

Pepper Jelly & Goat Cheese CAKES

Makes 24 cheesecakes   **Hands-on 14 minutes**
Total 2 hours, 44 minutes

Miniature paper baking cups
Vegetable cooking spray
¼ cup Italian-seasoned breadcrumbs
¼ cup ground toasted pecans
2 tablespoons grated Parmesan cheese
2 tablespoons butter, melted
6 ounces cream cheese, softened
1 (3-ounce) goat cheese log, softened
2 tablespoons milk
1 tablespoon Asian hot chili sauce (such as Sriracha)
1 large egg
¼ cup green pepper jelly
¼ cup red pepper jelly

1. Preheat oven to 350°F. Place paper baking cups in 2 (12-cup) miniature muffin pans, and coat with cooking spray. Stir together breadcrumbs and next 3 ingredients in a small bowl; firmly press about 1 teaspoon mixture in bottom of each baking cup.

2. Beat cream cheese and goat cheese at medium speed with an electric mixer until light and fluffy. Add milk and next 2 ingredients, beating just until blended. Spoon cheese mixture into baking cups, filling three-fourths full.

3. Bake at 350°F for 10 minutes or until set. Remove from oven to a wire rack, and cool completely (about 20 minutes). Remove from pans; place on a serving platter. Cover and chill 2 to 12 hours.

4. Microwave green pepper jelly in a small microwave-safe bowl at HIGH 20 to 25 seconds or until melted. Repeat procedure with red pepper jelly in another small microwave-safe bowl. Spoon 1 teaspoon melted green pepper jelly over each of 12 cheesecakes, and 1 teaspoon melted red pepper jelly over each of 12 remaining cheesecakes just before serving.

Espresso
SHORTBREAD
COOKIES

Makes about 4 dozen *Hands-on 45 minutes*
Total 3 hours, 15 minutes

1 cup butter, softened
½ cup granulated sugar
1 teaspoon sea salt
1 teaspoon vanilla extract
2 cups all-purpose flour
½ cup chocolate-covered espresso beans, chopped
1 tablespoon finely ground espresso beans
Wax paper
½ cup Demerara or turbinado sugar

1. Beat first 3 ingredients at medium speed with a heavy-duty electric stand mixer 2 to 3 minutes or until light and fluffy. Stir in vanilla.

2. Stir together flour and next 2 ingredients in a medium bowl. Gradually add to butter mixture, beating just until blended; stop to scrape bowl as needed. (Do not overmix.)

3. Divide dough in half. Turn 1 dough portion out onto wax paper, and shape into a 10- x 2-inch log. Sprinkle log with 3 tablespoons Demerara sugar, and roll log back and forth to adhere. Repeat with remaining dough portion and 3 tablespoons Demerara sugar. Wrap logs in plastic wrap, and chill 2 to 3 hours.

4. Preheat oven to 350°F. Cut chilled dough into ¼-inch-thick slices, and place 1 inch apart on 2 lightly greased baking sheets. Sprinkle 1½ teaspoons Demerara sugar over cookies on each sheet.

5. Bake, in batches, at 350°F for 12 to 15 minutes or until golden around edges, switching baking sheets halfway through.

6. Transfer to wire racks; cool 5 minutes. Serve immediately, or cool completely. Store in airtight container up to 4 days.

Chapter 5

SUNDAY UPSIDE DOWN

"So, waffles or pancakes tonight?" my mother would ask. My sister and I knew that question meant only one thing—our father was out of town. We couldn't think of a more magical meal than having breakfast for supper, a meal otherwise forbidden to be served in the evening. She learned waffle and pancake making from her father, a master of the iron and griddle. My grandfather would even gild the lily by serving a perfectly cooked over-light egg on the side.

These recipes can be served any time you like—as a delicious send-off for overnight guests, for brunch with friends, or as a special breakfast with the family. But serving these dishes for Sunday supper offers a pleasant surprise to close out the weekend.

Egg-and-bread casseroles and egg-and-vegetable stratas are easy on the cook, as they are prepared in advance and baked before serving. Waffles and pancakes are family favorites that really grab the limelight when served for supper. Grits cakes are a blank slate customizable with ingredients you have on hand—a canvas for your creativity.

Fruit salads both sweet and savory make Sunday supper a real meal. Tomatoes, cantaloupe, watermelon, and mango steal the scene as the stars of featured side dishes. Sprinkled throughout are cool and crisp beverages, both with and without alcohol, to quench the thirst of guests of any age.

On breakfast tables in some parts of the South, country ham with redeye gravy is just about as common as bacon. The origin of the name is debated, but the most common belief is that the gravy—a very thin, salty sauce—takes on a reddish tone from the browned bits scraped from the bottom of the skillet. Some Southerners make their gravy with water, others with coffee or cola. Lemon-poppy seed waffles are a Sunday supper treat, especially when made in a Belgian-style waffle maker. Blackberry Maple Syrup finds a perfect home in the big pockets the waffle maker creates. If you use a regular waffle iron, reduce the amount of batter to ½ cup per waffle. The mint lemonade is a perfectly puckery drink to cut the sweetness of the meal.

Prepare the waffles and keep them warm in a 200°F oven while using up all of the batter. The country ham is a last-minute prep, as is the lemonade. Freeze any leftover waffles to re-warm in a toaster for a quick weekday morning treat.

Lemon – Poppy Seed
BELGIAN WAFFLES
with Blackberry Maple Syrup

Serves 4   *Hands-on 20 minutes*   *Total 23 minutes*

LEMON-POPPY SEED BELGIAN WAFFLES
2 cups all-purpose baking mix
1 to 2 tablespoons poppy seeds
1 tablespoon lemon zest
1¼ cups cold club soda
1 large egg, lightly beaten
¼ cup butter, melted

BLACKBERRY MAPLE SYRUP
½ cup maple syrup
1 (12-ounce) package frozen blackberries, thawed
1 teaspoon lemon zest
2 teaspoons lemon juice

Vanilla yogurt (optional)

1. To prepare Lemon-Poppy Seed Belgian Waffles, stir together baking mix, poppy seeds, and lemon zest. Whisk together club soda, egg, and butter in a small bowl; gently whisk egg mixture into poppy seed mixture. (Mixture will be lumpy.) Let stand 3 minutes.

2. Cook batter according to manufacturer's instructions in a preheated, oiled Belgian-style waffle iron until golden (about ¾ to 1 cup batter per waffle).

3. To prepare Blackberry Maple Syrup, combine all ingredients in a medium bowl. Warm in microwave, if desired.

4. Pour syrup over waffles. Top with vanilla yogurt, if desired.

COUNTRY HAM
with Redeye Gravy

Serves 6   *Hands-on 20 minutes*   *Total 20 minutes*

1 pound country ham, cut into 3- x 4-inch pieces
2 tablespoons unsalted butter
1½ cups cola soft drink

1. Cook ham, in 3 batches, in a large stainless-steel skillet (do not use nonstick) over medium heat 4 to 5 minutes on each side or until browned. (The skillet will be dry.) Remove ham from skillet.

2. Melt butter in skillet. Stir in cola and ½ cup water, and simmer 3 minutes, stirring with a spatula to loosen particles from bottom of skillet. Serve hot gravy with ham.

The slow cooker does the work for this light and cheesy breakfast bread pudding. Dijon mustard gives the dish just a bit of zing. Ambrosia is a true Southern classic, and this version sticks with the basics of oranges and grapefruit but adds pineapple for a little tang and apples for crunch. The smoky, sticky, crunchy bacon cooks on the grill, but I've included oven directions as well.

Start the breakfast bread pudding in plenty of time to allow three or so hours cooking time. The citrus and pineapple can be sectioned and chopped a day ahead, but the apple should be added one to four hours ahead and sprinkled with lemon juice to prevent browning. If using canned or jarred fruit, save the juices and add them to the ambrosia. The bacon can be made ahead and reheated just before serving. Tie fresh rosemary sprigs to the handle of a wooden spoon with garden sisal or kitchen string, and use as an aromatic basting brush for the bacon.

Spinach-and-Broccoli Breakfast
BREAD PUDDING

Serves 8 to 10   *Hands-on 10 minutes*   *Total 3 hours, 20 minutes*

1 (10-ounce) package fresh baby spinach
Vegetable cooking spray
1 (1-pound) loaf Cuban bread, cut into 1-inch cubes
1 (10-ounce) package frozen broccoli florets, thawed
¼ cup chopped fresh chives
1 cup freshly grated Parmesan cheese
1 (12-ounce) can evaporated milk
1 cup milk
12 large eggs
3 tablespoons Dijon mustard
1 teaspoon kosher salt
¼ teaspoon ground red pepper
2 cups (8-ounces) shredded sharp Cheddar cheese

1. Place spinach and 1 tablespoon water in a large microwave-safe bowl. Cover with plastic wrap. Microwave at HIGH for 1 minute, and let stand, covered, until spinach is wilted. Drain well and chop.

2. Lightly grease a 6-quart slow cooker with cooking spray. Layer half of bread and all spinach, broccoli, and chives in slow cooker. Sprinkle with Parmesan cheese. Top with remaining bread cubes, pressing down gently to fit.

3. Whisk together evaporated milk and next 5 ingredients until frothy. Pour evenly over bread. Top with shredded cheese. Cover and cook on LOW for 3 to 4 hours or until set. Remove lid, and cook 10 minutes.

AMBROSIA
with Apples

Makes 8 cups   *Hands-on 45 minutes*
Total 1 hour, 45 minutes

4 oranges, peeled and sectioned
2 grapefruit, peeled and sectioned*
4 cups chopped fresh pineapple (about 1 small pineapple)
1 Fuji or Granny Smith apple, chopped
2 teaspoons fresh lemon juice
1 cup frozen grated coconut, thawed
¼ cup chopped fresh mint

1. Layer first 4 ingredients (in the order listed) in a large glass serving bowl or trifle dish. Sprinkle apple with lemon juice. Cover and chill 1 to 4 hours.

2. Sprinkle fruit mixture with coconut and mint. Gently toss just before serving.

*Blood oranges may be substituted.

Grilled
Balsamic – Molasses
BACON

Serves 6 to 8   *Hands-on 30 minutes*   *Total 1 hour*

14 (8-inch) wooden skewers
6 tablespoons molasses
3 tablespoons balsamic vinegar
¼ teaspoon ground red pepper
14 thick applewood-smoked bacon slices
3 fresh rosemary sprigs
Freshly ground black pepper

1. Soak wooden skewers in water 30 minutes. Preheat grill to 250° to 300°F (low) heat.

2. Stir together molasses and next 2 ingredients. Thread 1 bacon slice onto each skewer.

3. Grill bacon, covered with grill lid, 15 to 18 minutes or until bacon begins to brown, turning every 6 minutes. Baste with half of molasses mixture, using rosemary sprigs as a brush; grill, covered with grill lid, 5 minutes. Turn bacon, and baste with remaining molasses mixture, using rosemary sprigs. Grill, covered with grill lid, 5 minutes or until browned and crisp. Remove from grill. Sprinkle with freshly ground pepper to taste. Serve bacon immediately.

Not up for grilling? Place bacon on a rack in a parchment paper–lined rimmed baking sheet (without skewering). Bake in a 400°F oven for 15 to 18 minutes, or until desired doneness, basting as directed.

MENU THREE

SERVES 6-8

This hearty casserole feeds the whole family and is easy to prepare. The buttery biscuits layered with sausage, cheese, and green onions make for a savory and delicious meal. Lighten things up a bit with the citrus salad combining oranges, grapefruit, kiwi, and pomegranate seeds. Dressed with a mixture of honey and spices, it is as beautiful as it is tasty. These Bloody Marys get their kick from a barbecue rub; they're not too spicy, but have plenty of flavor.

The casserole takes about an hour from start to finish and is best served right out of the oven. The salad can be made up to a day ahead. Prepare as directed; cover and chill up to 24 hours. A pitcher of Bloody Marys can be made early and kept refrigerated until needed. Stir well before serving.

SAUSAGE BISCUIT GRAVY BAKE (page 257)

CITRUS SALAD WITH SPICED HONEY (page 258)

BARBECUE BLOODY MARY (page 260)

SET THE
SCENE

Sunday breakfast foods are welcome all day long.

Time this menu to serve shortly before houseguests depart from enjoying your weekend hospitality, whether it's midday, late afternoon, or evening. Or, serve it for supper with the family.

This beautifully rustic casserole served with a dazzling citrus salad is the perfect menu to accompany reminiscing about the weekend's highlights and making plans for the next get-together.

Spice things up with a Bloody Mary bar. We've got the recipe covered, so all you need to do is build the bar. Set ingredients out in bowls and provide a small cutting board, along with bamboo skewers, so guest can build their own garden-fresh swizzle sticks.

Here are some of our favorite additions:
· Lemons and limes
· Celery sticks and cucumber spears
· Stuffed olives
· Dill pickles
· Pickled okra and jalapeños
· Pearl onions and baby corn
· Marinated shrimp
· Crisp sliced bacon

For buffet dining, set the plates first in line. Next set the food with serving utensils. Have a basket of napkins and silverware at the end for easy pickup. You are all set for success.

Sausage Biscuit Gravy
BAKE

Serves 6 to 8 **Hands-on 20 minutes** *Total 1 hour*

1 pound ground pork sausage
2 teaspoons canola oil
5 tablespoons butter
¼ cup all-purpose flour
3 cups milk
¾ teaspoon salt
½ teaspoon freshly ground black pepper
Cooking spray
8 refrigerated jumbo biscuits
½ cup chopped green onions
¾ cup shredded sharp Cheddar cheese

1. Preheat oven to 350°F. Cook sausage in canola oil in a large skillet over medium-high heat 8 minutes or until crumbly and no longer pink; remove from skillet, and drain. Melt butter in skillet; whisk in flour. Whisk constantly 1 minute. Gradually whisk in milk, salt, and pepper. Bring to a boil, whisking constantly; cook 2 minutes. Stir in sausage.

2. Grease an 11- x 7-inch baking dish with cooking spray; place dish on a baking sheet. Split biscuits in half lengthwise; place 8 halves in baking dish. Top with half of sausage mixture and ¼ cup chopped green onions. Repeat layers. Sprinkle with ¾ cup shredded sharp Cheddar cheese. Bake at 350°F for 40 minutes or until golden.

SOUTHERN SAVVY
THE OVERNIGHT GUEST

Hosts will naturally make their guests comfortable. But what are the guest's responsibilities? Be clear about your comings and goings, arrival and departure times, and any scheduled time away from the house to see other local friends or business associates. Be sure to arrive with gifts. Gourmet treats and wine are always appreciated. If you are a returning guest, you may know of a specific need, such as a new set of coffee mugs or more wineglasses. If you've been invited to a vacation home, give a new board game or other rainy-day activity. New beach towels or comfy throws for the den are other good ideas.

CITRUS SALAD
with Spiced Honey

Serves 6 to 8   *Hands-on 30 minutes*   *Total 1 hour*

½ cup honey
1 (3-inch) cinnamon stick
1 bay leaf
1 teaspoon black peppercorns
¼ teaspoon dried crushed red pepper
4 whole cloves
3 medium-size oranges
3 mandarin oranges
2 Ruby Red grapefruit
2 limes
6 kumquats (optional)
1 (4.4-ounce) package fresh pomegranate seeds
Toppings: extra virgin olive oil, fresh mint leaves,
  sea salt

1. Bring first 6 ingredients and ½ cup water to a boil over medium-high heat. Boil, stirring often, 1 minute. Remove from heat, and let stand 30 minutes.

2. Meanwhile, peel oranges, next 3 ingredients, and, if desired, kumquats. Cut away bitter white pith. Cut each fruit into thin rounds. Arrange on a serving platter, and sprinkle with pomegranate seeds.

3. Pour honey mixture through a fine wire-mesh strainer, discarding solids. Drizzle fruit with desired amount of spiced honey; reserve remaining honey for another use (such as flavoring iced tea). Top with a drizzle of olive oil, a handful of mint leaves, and sea salt.

Use any combination of citrus to compose this vibrant, fresh salad.

Barbecue
BLOODY MARY

Serves 1   Hands-on 5 minutes
Total 10 minutes, including rub

Lime wedge
½ teaspoon Barbecue Rub
½ cup vegetable juice
1 tablespoon lime juice
1 teaspoon Worcestershire sauce
3 tablespoons vodka

Rub rim of an 8-ounce glass with a lime wedge; dip rim of glass in
¼ teaspoon Barbecue Rub to coat. Combine vegetable juice, lime
juice, Worcestershire sauce, vodka, and remaining ¼ teaspoon
Barbecue Rub in a cocktail shaker; fill with ice. Cover with lid; shake
vigorously until chilled. Strain into prepared glass filled with ice.

To serve 8, prepare recipe in a large pitcher with about 4 cups
veggie juice, ½ cup lime juice, 8 teaspoons Worcestershire sauce,
1½ cups (12 ounces) vodka, and 2 teaspoons Barbecue Rub.

Barbecue Rub

Hands-on 5 minutes   Total 5 minutes

2 tablespoons kosher salt
2 teaspoons paprika
1 teaspoon celery salt
½ teaspoon garlic powder
½ teaspoon freshly ground black pepper
¼ teaspoon ground red pepper

Stir together kosher salt, paprika, celery salt, garlic powder, ground
black pepper, and ground red pepper. Store in an airtight container.

*Try pepper vodka
for a little extra kick.*

SUNDAYS PAST & PRESENT
with SHERI CASTLE

Meet Sheri Castle, award-winning food writer and author of *The Southern Living Community Cookbook: Celebrating Food and Fellowship in the American South.*

HOMETOWN: Boone, NC **RESIDES:** Chapel Hill, NC

WHAT COMES TO MIND WHEN YOU THINK OF MEALS FROM SUNDAYS PAST?

Sunday meals for the Castle clan had two parts: a big Sunday dinner after church and a simple supper that evening. For dinner, all the aunts, uncles, and cousins converged at my grandparents' house. The table was set and the food spooned into our good dishes. We wore our Sunday clothes and were expected to muster up our manners. I adored those meals, but my best memories are of Sunday supper, which was casual, comfortable, and full of laughter.

WHAT DISH DID YOU LOOK FORWARD TO HAVING?

My favorite Sunday supper was when we had breakfast food, especially biscuits and gravy. My grandmother would split and toast any biscuits left from Sunday dinner and ladle on her thick, creamy, meaty gravy dusted with plenty of black pepper. When there was no leftover beef or chicken gravy from dinner, my grandmother made fantastic milk gravy from paper-thin slices of salty dried beef or pork breakfast sausage. I thought it was wonderful stuff. I still do and take considerable pride in my Castle skills as an accomplished "gravy whisperer."

TELL US ABOUT YOUR FAVORITE SUNDAY SUPPER—PAST OR PRESENT.

When I was a child, if my cousins and I were really lucky, we were allowed to eat Sunday supper in the den on TV trays. My favorite supper was homemade soup with buttered crackers and toasted cheese sandwiches. To this day, the thought of sipping soup and crushing saltines while watching *Lassie, Wild Kingdom,* and *Bonanza* makes me grin.

This frittata welcomes spring with my favorite veget[...]
stage. Trim the asparagus, discarding any tough parts of the stem. Chees[...]
favorite, and these get an extra boost from adding eggs and baking the casser[...]
more soufflé-like texture. Breakfast cookies are a dried-fruit-and-nut treat that ca[...]
early to stave off hunger or snatched up as a to-go snack.

Prepare the breakfast cookies a day ahead, as the dough needs to be well chilled before
baking. Omit drizzling with powdered sugar/cranberry mixture until serving. The cheese
grits casserole can be made ahead and reheated before serving, or timed to come out of the
oven as the frittata goes in. The frittata is best made just before serving.

Spring Vegetable
FRITTATA

Serves 4 to 6   **Hands-on 20 minutes**   **Total 36 minutes**

4 ounces fresh asparagus
½ (8-ounce) package cremini mushrooms, sliced
½ small yellow onion, sliced
1 tablespoon extra virgin olive oil
½ teaspoon kosher salt
½ teaspoon cracked black pepper
2 tablespoons butter
8 large eggs
2 ounces crumbled feta cheese

1. Preheat oven to 400°F. Cut asparagus into 1-inch pieces, discarding tough ends.

2. Sauté mushrooms and onion in 2 teaspoons hot oil in a 10-inch nonstick ovenproof skillet over medium heat 4 to 5 minutes or until onion is tender; remove from skillet. Add remaining 1 teaspoon oil to skillet, and sauté asparagus 2 to 3 minutes or until tender; stir in ¼ teaspoon each salt and pepper. Remove from skillet. Wipe skillet clean.

3. Melt butter in skillet over medium heat. Whisk together eggs and remaining ¼ teaspoon each salt and pepper. Add egg mixture to skillet. As eggs start to cook, gently lift edges of egg with a spatula, and tilt pan so uncooked portion flows underneath. Cook 2 to 3 minutes or until almost set. Top with vegetables and feta cheese.

4. Bake frittata at 400°F for 16 to 18 minutes or until lightly browned and puffy. Serve immediately.

Cheese Grits
CASSEROLE

Serves 6   Hands-on 20 minutes   Total 55 minutes

4 cups milk
¼ cup butter
1 cup uncooked quick-cooking grits
1 large egg, lightly beaten
2 cups (8 ounces) shredded sharp Cheddar cheese
1 teaspoon salt
½ teaspoon freshly ground black pepper
¼ cup grated Parmesan cheese

1. Preheat oven to 350°F. Bring milk just to a boil in a large saucepan over medium-high heat; gradually whisk in butter and grits. Reduce heat, and simmer, whisking constantly, 5 to 7 minutes or until grits are done. Remove from heat.

2. Stir in egg and next 3 ingredients. Pour into a lightly greased 11- x 7-inch baking dish. Sprinkle with grated Parmesan cheese.

3. Bake, covered, at 350°F for 35 to 40 minutes or until mixture is set. Serve immediately.

Breakfast COOKIES

Makes 10 cookies   Hands-on 20 minutes
Total 8 hours, 40 minutes

½ cup butter, softened
¼ cup honey
½ teaspoon salt
2 cups whole wheat flour
1 teaspoon vanilla extract
½ teaspoon baking soda
2 cups coarsely chopped assorted mixed nuts and dried fruit
Parchment paper
½ cup plus 2 tablespoons powdered sugar
1 tablespoon cranberry juice

1. Preheat oven to 325°F. Beat butter, honey, and salt at medium-low speed with an electric mixer until creamy. Add whole wheat flour, vanilla, and baking soda, and beat 1 minute or until blended. Stir in mixed nuts and dried fruit. Shape dough into a large log (about 3 inches in diameter); wrap in plastic wrap, and chill 8 hours to 1 week.

2. Cut dough into ½-inch-thick slices, and place on a parchment paper–lined baking sheet. Bake 20 minutes. Stir together powdered sugar and cranberry juice. Drizzle glaze over cookies.

MENU FIVE
SERVES 6

BLT BENEDICT WITH AVOCADO-TOMATO RELISH (PAGE 267)

ROASTED POTATOES (PAGE 268)

CREAMY FROZEN FRUIT POPS (PAGE 269)

The modern spin on eggs Benedict is freshened up with arugula and bacon and topped with an herbed avocado-tomato relish. Roasted potatoes help fill hungry tummies, and the fruit pops, made with fresh raspberries and strawberries, make you feel like a kid again.

The BLT Benedict needs a bit of attention due to the poaching of the eggs. Follow the tip to make the eggs ahead, if desired; sunny-side up or sliced boiled eggs would work just as well as poached eggs in this dish. The potatoes can be made up to a day ahead and reheated, or roasted to come out of the oven as the Benedicts are ready. Allow four hours for freezing these dairy-delightful fruit pops.

BLT BENEDICT
with Avocado-Tomato Relish

Serves 6   **Hands-on 15 minutes**   **Total 15 minutes**

1 cup halved grape tomatoes
1 avocado, diced
1 tablespoon chopped fresh basil
1 garlic clove, minced
2 tablespoons extra virgin olive oil
1 tablespoon red wine vinegar
6 large eggs
¼ cup mayonnaise
6 (¾-inch-thick) bakery bread slices, toasted
3 cups firmly packed arugula
12 thick bacon slices, cooked

1. Combine tomatoes, next 4 ingredients, salt and pepper to taste, and 2½ teaspoons red wine vinegar in a small bowl.

2. Add water to depth of 3 inches in a large saucepan. Bring to a boil; reduce heat, and maintain at a light simmer. Add remaining ½ teaspoon red wine vinegar. Break eggs, 1 at a time, and slip into water, as close as possible to surface. Simmer 3 to 5 minutes or to desired degree of doneness. Remove with a slotted spoon. Trim edges, if desired.

3. Spread mayonnaise on 1 side of each bread slice. Layer each with ½ cup arugula, 2 bacon slices, and 1 egg. Top with tomato mixture.

Immediately after poaching, place eggs in ice water, and refrigerate until serving time. Drain eggs; place in boiling water 45 seconds, and drain again. Serve immediately.

Roasted
POTATOES

Serves 6 to 8   *Hands-on 10 minutes*   *Total 50 minutes*

3 pounds baby red potatoes, quartered
1 tablespon peanut oil
1 teaspoon kosher salt

Preheat oven to 450°F. Stir together all ingredients in a large bowl.
Place potatoes in a single layer in a lightly greased 15- x 10-inch
jelly-roll pan. Bake at 450°F for 40 to 45 minutes or until tender and
browned, stirring twice.

Creamy Frozen
FRUIT POPS

Makes 10 pops   Hands-on 15 minutes
Total 4 hours, 15 minutes

1¼ cups frozen raspberries
1¼ cups sliced fresh strawberries
¼ cup honey
1 tablespoon fresh lemon juice
⅛ teaspoon salt
1 (7-ounce) container low-fat plain Greek yogurt
2 tablespoons buttermilk

Process raspberries, strawberries, honey, lemon juice, and salt in a food processor until smooth. Stir together yogurt and buttermilk. Fold yogurt mixture into berry mixture. Pour into 10 (2-ounce) pop molds. Top with lids; insert craft sticks, leaving 1½ to 2 inches sticking out of pop. Freeze 4 hours or until sticks are solidly anchored and pops are completely frozen.

MENU SIX

SERVES 6-8

Salty and sweet are a favorite combination, and that's just what this casserole delivers. It's a classic French toast egg casserole complete with pecans, butter, and syrup, but with the addition of salty ham. The cool and refreshing watermelon salad presents both red and yellow melon balls, chilled in a vodka and black raspberry liqueur syrup and topped with chopped mint. This sparkling punch recipe pairs tangy pink lemonade with tart cranberry juice for an irresistible combination. Assemble the casserole either the night before or at least eight hours before baking. The watermelon flesh can be removed in balls or cut into chunks and refrigerated a day ahead.

MAPLE HAM AND FRENCH TOAST CASSEROLE (page 273)

TIPSY RED-AND-YELLOW WATERMELON SALAD
(page 274)

SPARKLING PUNCH (page 276)

SET THE
SCENE

Repeating colors and blossoms in verdant hues lend freshness to the table.

The arrival of punch in the South predates that of the cocktail and was originally brought to us by the British—they were crazy for punch. Once it took hold in our region, it never let go. It's still a rare bridal or baby shower that doesn't include punch. The presence or absence of alcohol waxes and wanes through different time periods, but the consumption of punch is a mainstay for keeping cool. For this menu, put a fresh twist on the classic punch bowl and serve our sparkling punch from a Mason jar-inspired container with a silver ladle. Float lime slices for extra flavor, and add a tag to let guests know what you're serving.

The table setting can be as fussy or carefree as you are. These coordinating plates and colored glassware combine different hues, patterns, and sizes all in one place setting. The mint tinted chargers are used in lieu of place mats, and we've gathered vintage cocktail forks to hold the place card.

Let a unique find, such as this set of antique butter pats (tiny individual plates for serving butter), inspire your entire color palette. When topped with chilled butter curls, the dishes' delicate pattern will enliven the whole table. A collection of vases inspires these arrangements of hydrangea and viburnum blooms for a fresh look.

Maple Ham and French Toast
CASSEROLE

Serves 8 to 10   *Hands-on 15 minutes*   *Total 1 hour, plus 8 hours for chilling*

2 cups diced ham
Cooking spray
1 loaf French bread, sliced 1-inch thick
6 eggs
2 cups milk
¼ teaspoon ground nutmeg
½ cup dark brown sugar
3 tablespoons butter
½ cup maple syrup
1 cup chopped pecans
Blackberries (optional)
Whipped cream (optional)

1. Brown the ham over medium-high heat in a large skillet, and remove from pan to cool.

2. Coat a 9- x 13-inch baking dish with cooking spray. Line the bottom of the dish with bread slices. Stir together eggs, milk, nutmeg, and brown sugar. Pour over bread. Sprinkle with browned ham.

3. Cover casserole and chill 8 hours. When ready to bake, melt butter in a small saucepan, and stir in syrup and pecans. Pour over casserole, and place in cold oven. Bake at 400°F for 45 minutes, or until egg is set. Top with blackberries and whipped cream, if desired.

Buy whole spices and grind them as needed for the most flavor and freshness. A microplane grater makes easy work of grating whole nutmeg. Grate over a paper towel, then pour into measuring spoon to measure.

Tipsy Red–and–Yellow
WATERMELON SALAD

Serves 6 to 8   *Hands-on 20 minutes*   *Total 1 hour, 20 minutes*

½ (6-pound) red watermelon
½ (6-pound) yellow watermelon
1 cup fresh lemon juice (about 10 to 12 lemons)
⅔ cup sugar
½ cup vodka
⅓ cup black raspberry liqueur
Pinch of fine sea salt
1 tablespoon chopped fresh mint

1. Scoop watermelons into balls using various-size melon ballers, and place watermelon in a large bowl.

2. Whisk together lemon juice and next 4 ingredients in a medium bowl until sugar dissolves. Pour lemon juice mixture over watermelon balls; gently stir to coat. Cover and chill 1 to 2 hours.

3. Gently toss watermelon balls. Sprinkle with chopped fresh mint. Serve immediately with a slotted spoon.

Sparkling
PUNCH

Makes about 9 cups *Hands-on 5 minutes*
Total 1 hour, 5 minutes

1 (12-ounce) can frozen pink lemonade concentrate, thawed
4 cups white cranberry juice cocktail
1 quart club soda, chilled
Lemon slices (optional)

Stir together lemonade concentrate and cranberry juice cocktail in a large pitcher. Cover and chill at least 1 hour or up to 24 hours. Stir in club soda just before serving. Garnish with lemon slices, if desired.

Champagne *Punch*: Substitute 1 (750-milliliter) bottle extra-dry Champagne or sparkling wine and ¼ cup orange liqueur for club soda; proceed with recipe as directed.

SOUTHERN SAVVY
PLACE CARDS

Place cards are regaining popularity and can be used at any occasion, formal or informal. For a more formal occasion, heavy card stock is used. For an informal event, cards can remain formal or more relaxed—and creative! Most guests think the place card is solely there to guide them to their seat. Its secondary use is to help other guests remember your name. When writing the cards, use first names only if everyone clearly knows each other. Use first and last names when guests are meeting for the first time. I've found a third use: On the inside of a tented place card, I write one small helpful "job" that each guest can perform during the meal. Perhaps it is to clear a certain course or help dish up in the kitchen. It livens up a dinner party, and people truly enjoy having something specific to do in order to help the host.

SUNDAYS PAST & PRESENT
with REGINA CHARBONEAU

Meet Regina Charboneau, chef and author of *Regina's Table at Twin Oaks* and *Mississippi Current,* culinary director of the American Queen, owner of Twin Oaks Bed and Breakfast and King's Tavern in Natchez, MS.

HOMETOWN: Natchez, MS **RESIDES:** Natchez, MS

WHAT COMES TO MIND WHEN YOU THINK OF MEALS FROM SUNDAYS PAST?

Breakfast for supper. My mother, Frances Trosclair, was a great host but a terrible cook. The good food at our house was the product of our housekeeper, Alberta Fitzgerald, or my father, J.P. Trosclair, who came from a long line of wonderful cooks from South Louisiana. On Sunday evenings, my mother reluctantly took her turn in the kitchen. The one thing she could pull off was breakfast for supper. The menu was always the same: biscuits (not her own—I think from the A&P grocery store), pork sausage, and scrambled eggs. This simple Sunday supper was nothing more than satisfying. It was not the food but my mother's ease with each and every one of us, her laughter and calm spirit that seemed to settle us down after a busy weekend of activities and a house full of company. Our house was always filled with family and friends. There were rarely less than a dozen at the table, and most weekend meals had two dozen. I am one of nine children, and my parents had even more friends than children!

TELL US ABOUT YOUR FAVORITE SUNDAY SUPPER—PAST OR PRESENT.

My favorite Sunday supper is a more elegant version of my mother's. Biscuits for sure, but I serve my homemade butter biscuits, pan-fried quail with peppered bacon, shrimp in smoked tomato cream, and savory grits. As a filler, I include scrambled eggs with crème fraîche. I often prefer Champagne with this meal, but when I am serving a good red wine, I surround the eggs with an assortment of cheeses—always French. I cannot count the Sundays where friends have sat around my table until late in the evening at Twin Oaks. A memorable evening for me is always feeding my friends and a table filled with laughter and lively conversation. I always love those suppers that you just do not want to end. When you open your heart and home to family and friends, it really does not matter what you serve—that is gift enough, an important lesson I learned from my mother and father. I hope I have passed this love of Sunday suppers on to my sons.

We just can't get enough of overnight casseroles, and this praline-pecan version will look like a prom queen on your table. Plenty of pecans suspended in buttery brown sugar and maple syrup earn this dish its highly favorable rating. A fruit salad of melon and plums with a pepper-jelly vinaigrette cuts the sweetness of the casserole and is also an eye-catching addition to the table. Depending on the time of year, serve this adults-only coffee hot or over ice.

Assemble the casserole the night before or the morning of, depending on the serving time, allowing at least eight hours to chill before baking. The fruit can be cut and the vinaigrette made a day ahead, but combine them along with the watercress and feta cheese just before serving. The Coffee Milk Punch can be made a day ahead and refrigerated, then reheated if desired.

Praline–Pecan
FRENCH TOAST

Serves 8 to 10　　　　*Hands-on 20 minutes*　　　　*Total 8 hours, 55 minutes*

1 (16-ounce) French bread loaf
1 cup firmly packed light brown sugar
⅓ cup butter, melted
2 tablespoons maple syrup
¾ cup chopped pecans
4 large eggs, lightly beaten
1 cup milk
2 tablespoons granulated sugar
1 teaspoon ground cinnamon
1 teaspoon vanilla extract

1. Cut 10 (1-inch-thick) slices of bread. Reserve remaining bread for another use.

2. Stir together brown sugar and next 2 ingredients; pour into a lightly greased 13- x 9-inch baking dish. Sprinkle with chopped pecans.

3. Whisk together eggs and next 4 ingredients. Arrange bread slices over pecans; pour egg mixture over bread. Cover and chill 8 hours.

4. Preheat oven to 350°F. Bake bread at 350°F for 35 to 37 minutes or until golden brown. Serve immediately.

Melon and Plum
SALAD

Serves 6   Hands-on 20 minutes
Total 30 minutes, including vinaigrette

4 cups seeded and cubed watermelon
4 cups honeydew melon balls
3 red plums, sliced
2 cups torn watercress
1 cup crumbled feta cheese
Pepper Jelly Vinaigrette

Gently toss together first 5 ingredients, and place on a serving platter. Drizzle with vinaigrette, and season with salt and pepper to taste.

Pepper Jelly Vinaigrette

Makes about 1 cup   Hands-on 10 minutes
Total 10 minutes

¼ cup rice wine vinegar
¼ cup hot jalapeño pepper jelly
1 tablespoon chopped fresh mint
1 tablespoon grated onion
1 tablespoon fresh lime juice
¼ cup canola oil

Whisk together vinegar, pepper jelly, mint, onion, and lime juice. Gradually add canola oil in a slow, steady stream, whisking until smooth.

Coffee
MILK PUNCH

Makes 9 cups   *Hands-on 15 minutes*   *Total 15 minutes*

6 cups strong brewed hot coffee
½ cup hot fudge topping
¼ cup sugar
2 cups half-and-half
1 cup coffee liqueur
1 tablespoon vanilla extract

Whisk together hot coffee, fudge topping, and sugar in a large Dutch oven until smooth. Add half-and-half and remaining ingredients, stirring until blended. Bring mixture to a simmer over medium-high heat. Serve immediately, or let cool, cover, and chill 1 to 24 hours. Serve over ice.

Acknowledgments

Southern Living has entrusted me with their test-kitchen approved recipes, and it has been such a pleasure to present them to you as helpful menus. Sometimes thinking up which recipes to put together can be the hardest part of getting a meal to the table.

My thanks to my editor Katherine Cobbs and my project editor Lacie Pinyan for jumping in and bringing this book to life. I am grateful for their patience and professionalism. And thank you to Oxmoor House and Southern Living for this wonderful opportunity, and I hope there are many more collaborations in the future.

Meredith Butcher, I loved working with you. Thank you for getting this book off the ground.

Thank you to my many friends and colleagues in the culinary world, especially the ones nearest and dearest to my heart including Sheri Castle, Tamie Cook, Nathalie Dupree, Sandra Gutierrez, Nancie McDermott, and Virginia Willis. Your work inspires me every day.

My agent Lisa Ekus is a powerhouse and helps me claim my worth. Thank you.

Thank you to Anne for your unwavering support and love and for providing the most perfect place on this earth for a writer to write. Thank you for making it mine.

And thank you to my family with whom I have shared many Sunday suppers. You are my heart.

I dedicate this book to my grandmothers—Lorraine (Nana), who taught me all the Southern manners and proper hostess etiquette I would ever need to know, and Claudia (Nana Stuffie), who taught me all that really matters is platters of great food and an extra place at the table.

Join me online at www.cynthiagraubart.com

METRIC EQUIVALENTS

The recipes that appear in this cookbook use the standard U.S. method for measuring liquid and dry or solid ingredients (teaspoons, tablespoons, and cups). The information on this chart is provided to help cooks outside the United States successfully use these recipes. All equivalents are approximate.

USEFUL EQUIVALENTS FOR COOKING/OVEN TEMPERATURES

	FAHRENHEIT	CELSIUS	GAS MARK
FREEZE WATER	32° F	0° C	
ROOM TEMPERATURE	68° F	20° C	
BOIL WATER	212° F	100° C	
BAKE	325° F	160° C	3
	350° F	180° C	4
	375° F	190° C	5
	400° F	200° C	6
	425° F	220° C	7
	450° F	230° C	8
BROIL			GRILL

USEFUL EQUIVALENTS FOR LIQUID INGREDIENTS BY VOLUME

¼ tsp				=	1 ml
½ tsp				=	2 ml
1 tsp				=	5 ml
3 tsp	= 1 Tbsp		= ½ fl oz	=	15 ml
	2 Tbsp	= ⅛ cup	= 1 fl oz	=	30 ml
	4 Tbsp	= ¼ cup	= 2 fl oz	=	60 ml
	5⅓ Tbsp	= ⅓ cup	= 3 fl oz	=	80 ml
	8 Tbsp	= ½ cup	= 4 fl oz	=	120 ml
	10⅔ Tbsp	= ⅔ cup	= 5 fl oz	=	160 ml
	12 Tbsp	= ¾ cup	= 6 fl oz	=	180 ml
	16 Tbsp	= 1 cup	= 8 fl oz	=	240 ml
	1 pt	= 2 cups	= 16 fl oz	=	480 ml
	1 qt	= 4 cups	= 32 fl oz	=	960 ml
			33 fl oz	=	1,000 ml = 1 l

METRIC EQUIVALENTS FOR DIFFERENT TYPES OF INGREDIENTS

STANDARD CUP	FINE POWDER (e.g., flour)	GRAIN (e.g., rice)	GRANULAR (e.g., sugar)	LIQUID SOLIDS (e.g., butter)	LIQUID (e.g., milk)
1	140 g	150 g	190 g	200 g	240 ml
¾	105 g	113 g	143 g	150 g	180 ml
⅔	93 g	100 g	125 g	133 g	160 ml
½	70 g	75 g	95 g	100 g	120 ml
⅓	47 g	50 g	63 g	67 g	80 ml
¼	35 g	38 g	48 g	50 g	60 ml
⅛	18 g	19 g	24 g	25 g	30 ml

USEFUL EQUIVALENTS FOR DRY INGREDIENTS BY WEIGHT

To convert ounces to grams, multiply the number of ounces by 30.

1 oz	=	1/16 lb	=	30 g
4 oz	=	¼ lb	=	120 g
8 oz	=	½ lb	=	240 g
12 oz	=	¾ lb	=	360 g
16 oz	=	1 lb	=	480 g

USEFUL EQUIVALENTS FOR LENGTH

To convert inches to centimeters, multiply the number of inches by 2.5.

1 in	=			2.5 cm	
6 in	=	½ ft	=	15 cm	
12 in	=	1 ft	=	30 cm	
36 in	=	3 ft	= 1 yd =	90 cm	
40 in	=			100 cm	= 1 m

RECIPE INDEX

MENU INDEX